Oral Roberts

THE NEW TESTAMENT COMES ALIVE

A Personal New Testament Commentary

VOLUME THREE
HEBREWS - REVELATION

Table of
Contents

The Epistle
of Paul the
Apostle to the
Hebrews

The Epistle of Paul the Apostle to the

Hebrews

The book of Hebrews is more than a letter. It is a treatise written to a group of Hebrew Christians who were in the midst of terrible persecution. They were persecuted by their own people, the Jews, because they became Christians, and they were persecuted by the Romans who hated both Jews and Christians. We believe this happened after A.D. 64 when the Roman emperor Nero burned Rome, and just before A.D. 70 when the Roman general Titus destroyed Jerusalem, dispersing the Jews to the ends of the earth.

We are not told who wrote the book of Hebrews. Many people, myself included, believe St. Paul wrote it to the Hebrew Christians in Jerusalem after James, the head of the church, had been killed. I believe Paul was the only person qualified to write the book of Hebrews because he understood both the Hebrew faith and the Christian faith better than anyone else. No one understood the Old Testament origins of our faith as he did. And no one could compare with his understanding of Jesus and Him revealed in the flesh to man. But the important thing to remember is that God inspired the writing of this great book, the book of Hebrews.

The Hebrews this book was written to were second-generation Christians. They were led to Christ by those who had seen and heard Him themselves. But most of the original eyewitnesses had long since died. So the author was writing to a second-generation group, trying to show them the superiority of the Christian faith over the law of Moses and the Hebrew doctrines of the Old Testament. He was not trying to abolish the law, but show that it was an arrow pointing to the coming of the Messiah, Jesus Christ the Son of God.

Hebrews 1:1-3

God, who at sundry times and in divers manners spake in time past

> unto the fathers by the prophets, hath in these last days spoken unto us by his Son, whom he hath appointed heir of all things, by whom also he made the worlds; who being the brightness of his glory, and the express image of his person, and upholding all things by the word of his power, when he had by himself purged our sins, sat down on the right hand of the Majesty on high: . . .

The writer says God spoke in times past unto the fathers by the prophets. He is talking about the ancient fathers — the 12 sons of Jacob and their descendants who were the children of Israel. He also is talking about the Old Testament prophets. In Amos 3:7 we are told God does nothing without revealing His secrets first to His prophets. So he has something in mind.

He is going to show how the Son, Jesus Christ, is greater than the prophets. He says, "In the old days it was prophets like Elijah, Elisha, and Isaiah that God spoke to. But He has spoken to us in these last days by His own Son who is over the prophets. The Son is the heir of all things and by Him God sustains the world. He is exactly what our Father is like because He is the brightness of His glory and the express image of His personality. And He is seated at the right hand of our heavenly Father."

Hebrews 1:4

> Being made so much better than the angels, as he hath by inheritance obtained a more excellent name than they.

Jesus Greater Than Prophets and Angels

The writer is showing that Jesus Christ is not only greater than the prophets, He is greater than the angels also. He is saying, "You just remember there is a new name. And that name is above the prophets' names and above the angels' names. It is a name that is above everything that is named in this world and the world to come."

Hebrews 1:5-12

> For unto which of the angels said he at any time, Thou art my son, this day have I begotten thee? And again, I will be to him a Father, and he shall be to me a Son? And again, when he bringeth in the firstbegotten into the world, he saith, And let all the angels of God worship him. And of the angels he saith, Who maketh his angels spirits, and his ministers a flame of fire.
>
> But unto the Son he saith, Thy throne, O God, is for ever and ever: a sceptre of righteousness is the sceptre of thy kingdom. Thou hast

loved righteousness, and hated iniquity; therefore God, even thy God, hath anointed thee with the oil of gladness above thy fellows. And, Thou, Lord, in the beginning hast laid the foundation of the earth; and the heavens are the works of thine hands: they shall perish; but thou remainest; and they all shall wax old as doth a garment; and as a vesture shalt thou fold them up, and they shall be changed: but thou art the same, and thy years shall not fail.

The writer is referring to certain Old Testament Scriptures describing the Son of God. He is illustrating how much greater the Son of God is than the prophets and angels. The Son of God is eternal, He will never change, and His years shall never fail.

Hebrews 1:13-2:4

But to which of the angels said he at any time, Sit on my right hand, until I make thine enemies thy footstool? Are they not all ministering spirits, sent forth to minister for them who shall be heirs of salvation? Therefore we ought to give the more earnest heed to the things which we have heard, lest at any time we should let them slip. For if the word spoken by angels was stedfast, and every transgression and disobedience received a just recompence of reward; how shall we escape, if we neglect so great salvation; which at the first began to be spoken by the Lord, and was confirmed unto us by them that heard him; God also bearing them witness, both with signs and wonders, and with divers miracles, and gifts of the Holy Ghost, according to his own will?

Another reason I believe Paul wrote Hebrews is that the writer says the word "was confirmed unto us by them that heard him." As far as we know, Paul never saw Jesus Christ. He did not know Him face to face as Peter, James, and John did. But he received the revelation from the Lord and later was commended by the apostles themselves.

Hebrews 2:5-8

For unto the angels hath he not put in subjection the world to come, whereof we speak. But one in a certain place testified, saying, What is man, that thou art mindful of him? or the son of man, that thou visitest him? Thou madest him a little lower than the angels; thou crownedst him with glory and honour, and didst set him over the works of thy hands: Thou hast put all things in subjection under his feet. For in that he put all in subjection under him, he left nothing that is not put under him. But now we see not yet all things put under him.

The writer is saying that God did not make the angels as the ones who were to rule. For in Genesis 1:28 He gave man authority over all created things. It was man who was originally given control over the earth, although we do not see that fully evidenced today.

Hebrews 2:9

> But we see Jesus, who was made a little lower than the angels for the suffering of death, crowned with glory and honour; that he by the grace of God should taste death for every man.

In order for Jesus to be born of a woman He had to be made a little lower than the angels. He therefore could experience death for all people and thereby open the door for our reconciliation with God.

Hebrews 2:10

> For it became him, for whom are all things, and by whom are all things, in bringing many sons unto glory, to make the captain of their salvation perfect through sufferings.

The word "perfect" here means "fully adequate." My friend, Christ was fully adequate to do His work. For He became flesh of our flesh, bone of our bone, He sat where we sit, and He experienced what we experience in every way. So it was through experiencing all our sufferings that He became fully adequate, perfect, for the work the Father sent Him to do.

Hebrews 2:11-15

> For both he that sanctifieth and they who are sanctified are all of one: for which cause he is not ashamed to call them brethren, saying, I will declare thy name unto my brethren, in the midst of the church will I sing praise unto thee. And again, I will put my trust in him. And again, Behold I and the children which God hath given me.
> Forasmuch then as the children are partakers of flesh and blood, he also himself likewise took part of the same; that through death he might destroy him that had the power of death, that is, the devil; and deliver them who through fear of death were all their lifetime subject to bondage.

The writer is saying Jesus Christ brought deliverance so that we as Christians will have no fear of death. Death is but a moment through which we pass from this life into the life to come with God.

Hebrews 2:16-18

> For verily he took not on him the nature of angels; but he took on

> him the seed of Abraham. Wherefore in all things it behoved him to
> be made like unto his brethren, that he might be a merciful and faithful
> high priest in things pertaining to God, to make reconciliation for the
> sins of the people. For in that he himself hath suffered being tempted,
> he is able to succour them that are tempted.

Jesus Christ is shown as the one who took the place of the ancient high priest. He is fully able to reconcile us to God because He is fully man and yet fully God. He suffered through His temptations but He did not give in. Therefore, He is able to deliver us so that we will never give in either.

We have seen that Jesus is superior to the prophets and the angels. In the third chapter of Hebrews the writer will prove that Jesus is superior to Moses. Why is that so important? Because the Jews thought Moses was the greatest of all. Moses talked face to face with God. He was the man God used to deliver the children of Israel from Egypt. He was given the Ten Commandments. To the Jew, no one was greater than Moses.

Hebrews 3:1-6

> Wherefore, holy brethren, partakers of the heavenly calling, consider
> the Apostle and High Priest of our profession, Christ Jesus; who was
> faithful to him that appointed him, as also Moses was faithful in all
> his house. For this man was counted worthy of more glory than Moses,
> inasmuch as he who hath builded the house hath more honour than
> the house. For every house is builded by some man; but he that built
> all things is God. And Moses verily was faithful in all his house, as a
> servant, for a testimony of those things which were to be spoken
> after; but Christ as a son over his own house; whose house are we,
> if we hold fast the confidence and the rejoicing of the hope firm unto
> the end.

The writer is saying that Moses did not create the law or give the Ten Commandments. He did not build the household of Israel. He did not speak of himself, because he was the servant. But Jesus Christ spoke of himself. Jesus Christ went to the cross and rose from the dead. And He is building the family of God himself and He is greater than Moses.

Hebrews 3:7-19

> Wherefore (as the Holy Ghost saith, To day if ye will hear his voice,
> harden not your hearts, as in the provocation, in the day of temptation
> in the wilderness: when your fathers tempted me, proved me, and
> saw my works forty years. Wherefore I was grieved with that

generation, and said, They do alway err in their heart; and they have not known my ways. So I sware in my wrath, They shall not enter into my rest.)

Take heed, brethren, lest there be in any of you an evil heart of unbelief, in departing from the living God. But exhort one another daily, while it is called To day; lest any of you be hardened through the deceitfulness of sin. For we are made partakers of Christ, if we hold the beginning of our confidence stedfast unto the end; while it is said, To day if ye will hear his voice, harden not your hearts, as in the provocation.

For some, when they had heard, did provoke: howbeit not all that came out of Egypt by Moses. But with whom was he grieved forty years? was it not with them that had sinned, whose carcasses fell in the wilderness? And to whom sware he that they should not enter into his rest, but to them that believed not? So we see that they could not enter in because of unbelief.

The Sin of Unbelief

The writer is coming to the main point he has been leading up to — keeping the heart open rather than hardening it against God. He reminds the Jewish Christians of something they have known about since childhood — the fact that God had a difficult time with the children of Israel because of their unbelief. He says, "Please do not let the same thing happen to you that happened to them. They did not take God at His word in the wilderness. They had plenty of evidence for their faith to rest on, but they shoved it aside and went into unbelief. I do not want you Hebrew Christians to do the same thing, because there is a rest of God waiting for you. It is yours, if you will only stay in belief."

Hebrews 4:1-6

Let us therefore fear, lest, a promise being left us of entering into his rest, any of you should seem to come short of it. For unto us was the gospel preached, as well as unto them: but the word preached did not profit them, not being mixed with faith in them that heard it. For we which have believed do enter into rest, as he said, As I have sworn in my wrath, if they shall enter into my rest: although the works were finished from the foundation of the world. For he spake in a certain place of the seventh day on this wise, And God did rest the seventh day from all his works. And in this place again, If they shall enter into my rest.

Seeing therefore it remaineth that some must enter therein, and they to whom it was first preached entered not in because of unbelief . . .

In describing the rest available to the Christian through his faith, the writer uses the illustration of God resting on the seventh day of creation. He says God is offering that completeness of rest, or inner peace, to His people. Therefore, we should beware, lest having these promises, we set them aside by disobedience in the same way the children of Israel did in the past.

Hebrews 4:7-10
> Again, he limited a certain day, saying in David, To day, after so long a time; as it is said, To day if ye will hear his voice, harden not your hearts. For if Jesus had given them rest, then would he not afterward have spoken of another day.
>
> There remaineth therefore a rest to the people of God. For he that is entered into his rest, he also hath ceased from his own works, as God did from his.

The writer is saying that there remains a rest for the people of God through Jesus Christ. God has continually given us an opportunity to enter that rest by saying, "Today, if you hear His voice, harden not your heart." And the reward of entering is peace, the peace of knowing we are one with God and He is taking care of our lives.

Hebrews 4:11-13
> Let us labour therefore to enter into that rest, lest any man fall after the same example of unbelief. For the word of God is quick, and powerful, and sharper than any two-edged sword, piercing even to the dividing asunder of soul and spirit, and of the joints and marrow, and is a discerner of the thoughts and intents of the heart. Neither is there any creature that is not manifest in his sight: but all things are naked and opened unto the eyes of him with whom we have to do.

God's Two-edged Sword

The writer is saying that we are to be very careful lest we fall into the same unbelief and disobedience the Israelites did because no matter how they tried to conceal their unbelief, God's Word was quick. That is, it had the effective power of revealing what was in their hearts. He mentions the dividing of joints and marrow because he knows these Jewish people understand the Old Testament teaching that through the marrow blood is created and in it is the essence of physical life.

Therefore, the Word comes right through the total being of a person and reveals him as he is. Even the intents of his heart are made clear so that nothing is hidden from God. No matter how small it may be it is revealed before the eyes of Him with whom we have to deal. Consequently, we must not be caught up in unbelief and disobedience because God's Word will reveal the condition of our hearts.

Hebrews 4:14-16

> Seeing then that we have a great high priest, that is passed into the heavens, Jesus the Son of God, let us hold fast our profession. For we have not an high priest which cannot be touched with the feeling of our infirmities; but was in all points tempted like as we are, yet without sin. Let us therefore come boldly unto the throne of grace, that we may obtain mercy, and find grace to help in time of need.

Our Great High Priest

As Christians we see Jesus in a different light than the Hebrews saw the high priest of the old covenant who was separate from the people. For although he was chosen from the people and was their mediator, he was entirely separate. He went alone into the Holy of Holies carrying the blood of an animal sacrifice he substituted for the people's sins.

Jesus, however, was not one degree removed from us. He went through this world as a human being, experienced every type of temptation any human has ever experienced, returned to the Father, and through His Spirit comes back to us so we can touch Him with our faith. Therefore, we can go with a personal boldness to the throne of grace, which is Jesus Christ himself, that we may obtain deliverance in our time of need.

Hebrews 5:1-10

> For every high priest taken from among men is ordained for men in things pertaining to God, that he may offer both gifts and sacrifices for sins: who can have compassion on the ignorant, and on them that are out of the way; for that he himself also is compassed with infirmity. And by reason hereof he ought, as for the people, so also for himself, to offer for sins. And no man taketh this honour unto himself, but he that is called of God, as was Aaron.
>
> So also Christ glorified not himself to be made an high priest; but he that said unto him, Thou art my son, to day have I begotten thee. As he saith also in another place, Thou art a priest for ever after the order of Melchisedec. Who in the days of his flesh, when he had

offered up prayers and supplications with strong crying and tears unto him that was able to save him from death, and was heard in that he feared; though he were a Son, yet learned he obedience by the things which he suffered; and being made perfect, he became the author of eternal salvation unto all them that obey him; called of God an high priest after the order of Melchisedec.

The writer to the Hebrews is taking a fourth step. First, he established the fact that the Son of God is greater than the prophets. Second, He is greater than the angels. Third, He is greater than Moses. Fourth, He is greater than the first high priest and the whole priest system.

Think back with me to the book of Genesis and to Abraham, whom God called from Ur of the Chaldees and told to go to the land He would give him and his descendants, the land we know as the land of Israel. When Abraham arrived there he discovered a man by the name of Melchisedec who was a priest of righteousness and the king of Salem (which later became Jerusalem). He was an unusually great man. The Bible teaches he was even greater than Abraham, the founder of the Hebrews' faith. So when Abraham recognized Melchisedec for who he was, he gave him tithes of all he possessed. In essence, Melchisedec became the priest of Abraham. It is after the order of this man, a man greater than even Abraham himself, that Christ became our high priest.

Hebrews 5:11-6:8

Of whom we have many things to say, and hard to be uttered, seeing ye are dull of hearing. For when for the time ye ought to be teachers, ye have need that one teach you again which be the first principles of the oracles of God; and are become such as have need of milk, and not of strong meat. For every one that useth milk is unskilful in the word of righteousness: for he is a babe. But strong meat belongeth to them that are of full age, even those who by reason of use have their senses exercised to discern both good and evil.

Therefore leaving the principles of the doctrine of Christ, let us go on unto perfection; not laying again the foundation of repentance from dead works, and of faith toward God, of the doctrine of baptisms, and of laying on of hands, and of resurrection of the dead, and of eternal judgment. And this will we do, if God permit.

For it is impossible for those who were once enlightened, and have tasted of the heavenly gift, and were made partakers of the Holy Ghost, and have tasted the good word of God, and the powers of the world to come, if they shall fall away, to renew them again unto repentance; seeing they crucify to themselves the Son of God afresh, and put him to an open shame.

For the earth which drinketh in the rain that cometh oft upon it, and bringeth forth herbs meet for them by whom it is dressed, receiveth blessing from God: but that which beareth thorns and briers is rejected, and is nigh unto cursing; whose end is to be burned.

Maturity and Apostasy

The writer says to the Hebrew Christians, "It is time that we leave the basic principles of the doctrine of Christ. We cannot continually stay only in them. It is time for us to go forward into spiritual maturity." Then he mentions five things he considers the fundamentals of our faith: repentance and faith toward God, the doctrine of water baptism, the laying on of hands to commission for Christian service and to receive the Holy Spirit, the doctrine of the resurrection of the dead, and eternal judgment for those who reject Christ. In other words, there is much more to Christianity than these five principles. These are necessary, but we must move on in our walk with Christ.

The writer also says that for individuals who become apostate and fall away from Christ, there is no possibility of renewal in Him. (Let me remind you that Hebrews was written at a time of great persecution. There was a lot of apostasy taking place because all a believer in Christ had to do was deny Jesus Christ as Lord, and he would not be persecuted). Therefore, people who are apostates are not mere backsliders. The backslider can always come back to God if he does not wait too long. But the apostate is different. He denies what he once knew. He takes these principles of Christ and rejects them totally and eternally. In his heart of hearts he makes an eternal choice and, therefore, there is no one who can save him or bring him back. He has removed Christ from his life forever and ever.

Hebrews 6:9-15

But, beloved, we are persuaded better things of you, and things that accompany salvation, though we thus speak. For God is not unrighteous to forget your work and labour of love, which ye have shewed toward his name, in that ye have ministered to the saints, and do minister. And we desire that every one of you do shew the same diligence to the full assurance of hope unto the end: that ye be not slothful, but followers of them who through faith and patience inherit the promises.

For when God made promise to Abraham, because he could swear by no greater, he sware by himself, saying, Surely blessing I will bless thee, and multiplying I will multiply thee. And so, after he had patiently endured, he obtained the promise.

The writer is taking us back to the days of Abraham when God made promises to him. God told him if he would trust His word and simply follow Him by faith alone, He would bless and multiply him. It took a lot of patience, a lot of hard work, and a lot of waiting, but Abraham obtained the promise.

Hebrews 6:16-20
> For men verily swear by the greater: and an oath for confirmation is to them an end of all strife.
> Wherein God, willing more abundantly to shew unto the heirs of promise the immutability of his counsel, confirmed it by an oath: that by two immutable things, in which it was impossible for God to lie, we might have a strong consolation, who have fled for refuge to lay hold upon the hope set before us: which hope we have as an anchor of the soul, both sure and steadfast, and which entereth into that within the veil; whither the forerunner is for us entered, even Jesus, made an high priest for ever after the order of Melchisedec.

The writer is saying that the most glorious things of life and the world to come are promised to you and me as believers. For not only did God promise it once, He made a double promise by swearing by himself. He also says when Christ was crucified, the veil in the temple in Jerusalem, which separated the holy from the most holy, was split. It was taken away, meaning that the wall of separation people felt from God has vanished, and Jesus has come directly into our lives.

Hebrews 7:1-3
> For this Melchisedec, king of Salem, priest of the most high God, who met Abraham returning from the slaughter of the kings, and blessed him; to whom also Abraham gave a tenth part of all; first being by interpretation King of righteousness, and after that also King of Salem, which is, King of peace; without father, without mother, without descent, having neither beginning of days, nor end of life; but made like unto the Son of God; abideth a priest continually.

We are told something very special about Melchisedec — he was without father or mother, having neither beginning of days nor end of life. That does not mean he did not have a human father, mother, or human descent. It simply means God intended for us to understand this man was selected by Him to be separate and different from all other human beings so he could be a priest eternally and continually.

Hebrews 7:4-10

> Now consider how great this man was, unto whom even the patriarch Abraham gave the tenth of the spoils. And verily they that are of the sons of Levi, who receive the office of the priesthood, have a commandment to take tithes of the people according to the law, that is, of their brethren, though they come out of the loins of Abraham: but he whose descent is not counted from them received tithes of Abraham, and blessed him that had the promises. And without all contradiction the less is blessed of the better.
>
> And here men that die receive tithes; but there he receiveth them, of whom it is witnessed that he liveth. And as I may so say, Levi also, who received tithes, payed tithes in Abraham. For he was yet in the loins of his father, when Melchisedec met him.

The response of Abraham's faith to God through tithing was so great that it spiritually affected his unborn sons and daughters who became the children of Israel.

Hebrews 7:11-19

> If therefore perfection were by the Levitical priesthood, (for under it the people received the law,) what further need was there that another priest should rise after the order of Melchisedec, and not be called after the order of Aaron? For the priesthood being changed, there is made of necessity a change also of the law. For he of whom these things are spoken pertaineth to another tribe, of which no man gave attendance at the altar. For it is evident that our Lord sprang out of Judah; of which tribe Moses spake nothing concerning priesthood.
>
> And it is yet far more evident: for that after the similitude of Melchisedec there ariseth another priest, who is made, not after the law of a carnal commandment, but after the power of an endless life. For he testifieth, Thou art a priest for ever after the order of Melchisedec.
>
> For there is verily a disannulling of the commandment going before for the weakness and unprofitableness thereof. For the law made nothing perfect, but the bringing in of a better hope did; by the which we draw nigh unto God.

One of the problems the Hebrew Christians were facing was the Judaizers trying to tell them that Jesus Christ could not be their priest because He did not descend from the tribe of Levi. The Judaizers always went back to that pedigree — you had to be born in direct line and have absolute proof of the fact you were a Levite in order to become a priest. So the writer is saying, "You are absolutely right. Jesus did not descend from Levi, He came from the tribe of Judah. But you have missed the whole point. He is not a priest after the order of the Levites who came into the priesthood by human pedigree. Jesus is a priest after the order of Melchisedec whose life is eternal."

Then the writer to the Hebrews says in Verse 19, "The law of Moses made nothing perfect. First, it showed us a sense of sin, and then it revealed our need of a Redeemer. But it was never complete in itself." The 19th verse may in fact be the key verse to the whole book, for it is through Jesus Christ that we draw near to God. Therefore, the writer is telling the Hebrew Christians, "Do not go back to the old system. You have Jesus Christ who is after the order of Melchisedec and is a priest forever. He is in your hearts, your spirits, and your minds. Through Him you can draw nigh to God. Do not throw that away."

Hebrews 7:20-28

And inasmuch as not without an oath he was made priest: (For those priests were made without an oath; but this with an oath by him that said unto him, The Lord sware and will not repent, Thou art a priest for ever after the order of Melchisedec:) by so much was Jesus made a surety of a better testament.

And they truly were many priests, because they were not suffered to continue by reason of death: but this man, because he continueth ever, hath an unchangeable priesthood. Wherefore he is able also to save them to the uttermost that come unto God by him, seeing he ever liveth to make intercession for them.

For such an high priest became us, who is holy, harmless, undefiled, separate from sinners, and made higher than the heavens; who needeth not daily, as those high priests, to offer up sacrifice, first for his own sins, and then for the people's: for this he did once, when he offered up himself. For the law maketh men high priests which have infirmity; but the word of the oath, which was since the law, maketh the Son, who is consecrated for evermore.

The Priesthood of Jesus versus the Levitical Priesthood

There are three ways the priesthood of Jesus, with that of Melchisedec, is compared to the Levitical priesthood. First, Melchisedec became a priest by the order and high calling of God and not through his human pedigree. Jesus likewise was made a high priest through the calling of God. Second, Melchisedec did not have sons who carried on his priesthood as Levi did. He was a symbol of an eternal priesthood. Jesus' priesthood is the same. Third, we have no record of Melchisedec having to offer a sacrifice first for his own sins, whereas in the Levitical priesthood the high priest had to offer a sacrifice for his own sins before he could offer up a sacrifice for the sins of the people. And Jesus did not go to the cross for himself because He had no sin. He went there to offer himself up as the sacrifice for our sins. Therefore, Jesus Christ is able to save to the uttermost. There is nothing about our lives He cannot save.

Hebrews 8:1-10

Now of the things which we have spoken this is the sum: We have such an high priest, who is set on the right hand of the throne of the Majesty in the heavens; a minister of the sanctuary, and of the true tabernacle, which the Lord pitched, and not man.

For every high priest is ordained to offer gifts and sacrifices: wherefore it is of necessity that this man have somewhat also to offer. For if he were on earth, he should not be a priest, seeing that there are priests that offer gifts according to the law: who serve unto the example and shadow of heavenly things, as Moses was admonished of God when he was about to make the tabernacle: for, See, saith he, that thou make all things according to the pattern shewed to thee in the mount.

But now hath he obtained a more excellent ministry, by how much also he is the mediator of a better covenant, which was established upon better promises. For if that first covenant had been faultless, then should no place have been sought for the second.

For finding fault with them, he saith, Behold, the days come, saith the Lord, when I will make a new covenant with the house of Israel and with the house of Judah: not according to the covenant that I made with their fathers in the day when I took them by the hand to lead them out of the land of Egypt; because they continued not in my covenant, and I regarded them not, saith the Lord. For this is the covenant that I will make with the house of Israel after those days, saith the Lord; I will put my laws into their mind, and write them in their hearts: and I will be to them a God, and they shall be to me a people: . . .

A Better Covenant

The writer to the Hebrew Christians is emphasizing the word

"better." He is saying, "Jesus is better. There is a better promise, a better covenant, a better hope, a better priesthood, a better mediator, a better resurrection, a better heaven, and a better life here on earth and in the world to come."

He points out very carefully that Jeremiah and David both looked forward to a new covenant because they knew the first covenant had been broken, not by God but by the people. And once the covenant was broken, it became of no effect. So God promises a new covenant not built so much upon externals, but one He would write into the hearts and minds of His people. It will be a covenant so effective that He will be all He can be as God and we will be all we can be as His people. It will be an intimate, personal relationship that He has with us and that we have with Him. That is what the new covenant will be. And that is what the new covenant is through Jesus Christ our Lord.

Hebrews 8:11-9:15

And they shall not teach every man his neighbour, and every man his brother, saying, Know the Lord: for all shall know me, from the least to the greatest. For I will be merciful to their unrighteousness, and their sins and their iniquities will I remember no more.

In that he saith, A new covenant, he hath made the first old. Now that which decayeth and waxeth old is ready to vanish away.

Then verily the first covenant had also ordinances of divine service, and a worldly sanctuary. For there was a tabernacle made; the first, wherein was the candlestick, and the table, and the shewbread; which is called the sanctuary. And after the second vail, the tabernacle which is called the Holiest of all; which had the golden censer, and the ark of the covenant overlaid round about with gold, wherein was the golden pot that had manna, and Aaron's rod that budded, and the tables of the covenant; and over it the cherubims of glory shadowing the mercy seat; of which we cannot now speak particularly. Now when these things were thus ordained, the priests went always into the first tabernacle, accomplishing the service of God.

But into the second went the high priest alone once every year, not without blood, which he offered for himself, and for the errors of the people: the Holy Ghost this signifying, that the way into the holiest of all was not yet made manifest, while as the first tabernacle was yet standing: which was a figure for the time then present, in which were offered both gifts and sacrifices, that could not make him that did the service perfect, as pertaining to the conscience; which stood only in meats and drinks, and divers washings, and carnal ordinances, imposed on them until the time of reformation.

But Christ being come an high priest of good things to come, by a greater and more perfect tabernacle, not made with hands, that is to say, not of this building; neither by the blood of goats and calves, but by his own blood he entered in once into the holy place, having obtained eternal redemption for us. For if the blood of bulls and of goats, and the ashes of an heifer sprinkling the unclean, sanctifieth to the purifying of the flesh: how much more shall the blood of Christ, who through the eternal Spirit offered himself without spot to God, purge your conscience from dead works to serve the living God?

And for this cause he is the mediator of the new testament, that by means of death, for the redemption of the transgressions that were under the first testament, they which are called might receive the promise of eternal inheritance.

Because Jesus Christ came, the Hebrew Christians (and we, too) do not need a tabernacle or tent like Moses had fashioned. For Christ is in a tabernacle made with hands; He actually lives in our hearts. And if the blood of bulls and goats was offered as a sacrifice for the sins of the people, how much more will the actual blood of Christ be sufficient to cleanse our conscience, to save our souls, and to bring us to the point where we can serve the living God?

Through the cross, Jesus became the mediator of a new covenant. He opened up a new covenant God had had in His mind from the beginning.

Hebrews 9:16-28

For where a testament is, there must also of necessity be the death of the testator. For a testament is of force after men are dead: otherwise it is of no strength at all while the testator liveth.

Whereupon neither the first testament was dedicated without blood. For when Moses had spoken every precept to all the people according to the law, he took the blood of calves and of goats, with water, and scarlet wool, and hyssop, and sprinkled both the book, and all the people, saying, This is the blood of the testament which God hath enjoined unto you. Moreover he sprinkled with blood both the tabernacle, and all the vessels of the ministry. And almost all things are by the law purged with blood; and without shedding of blood is no remission.

It was therefore necessary that the patterns of things in the heavens should be purified with these; but the heavenly things themselves with better sacrifices than these. For Christ is not entered into the holy places made with hands, which are the figures of the true; but into heaven itself, now to appear in the presence of God for us: nor yet that he should offer himself often, as the high priest entereth into the holy place every year with blood of others; for then must he often have suffered since the foundation of the world: but now once in the end of the world hath he appeared to put away sin by the sacrifice of himself.

And as it is appointed unto men once to die, but after this the judgment: so Christ was once offered to bear the sins of many; and unto them that look for him shall he appear the second time without sin unto salvation.

Why is the Bible a book of blood? Because from God's standpoint, life is in the blood. Blood is life. And life is the most precious thing in the world. So when Jesus came, God was giving the most precious thing of all, the life of His only begotten Son.

Notice Verses 27 and 28. We often take Verse 27 in isolation. It says, "And as it is appointed unto men once to die, but after death the judgment." We usually put a period there and make that a single statement by itself. But it is not. It hangs on the next verse, which says, "So Christ was once offered to bear the sins of many; and unto them that look for him shall he appear the second time without sin unto salvation."

It is true that death is an appointment and that after death there will be the judgment. But Christ is talking about something more than that. He is saying He has already dealt with sin. He has made himself a sacrifice to bear the sins of all mankind. So our attitude should be one of looking for Him because He will be our ultimate salvation.

Hebrews 10:1-10

For the law having a shadow of good things to come, and not the very image of the things, can never with those sacrifices which they offered year by year continually make the comers thereunto perfect. For then would they not have ceased to be offered? because that the worshippers once purged should have had no more conscience of sins. But in those sacrifices there is a remembrance again made of sins every year. For it is not possible that the blood of bulls and of goats should take away sins.

Wherefore when he cometh into the world, he saith, Sacrifice and offering thou wouldest not, but a body hast thou prepared me: in burnt offerings and sacrifices for sin thou hast had no pleasure. Then said I, Lo, I come (in the volume of the book it is written of me,) to do thy will, O God.

Above when he said, Sacrifice and offering and burnt offerings and offering for sin thou wouldest not, neither hadst pleasure therein; which are offered by the law; then said he, Lo, I come to do thy will, O God. He taketh away the first, that he may establish the second.

By the which will we are sanctified through the offering of the body
of Jesus Christ once for all.

If we had lived under the old covenant, we would have had to
look forward every year to the time when the high priest went into
the Holy of Holies to present the blood sacrifice which would roll
our sins away one more year. In our minds we would have known
we would have to come back a year later and the year after that
and the year after that for the rest of our lives.

But when Jesus came He settled the sin question once and for
all. We do not have to go back once a year to make an atonement
for our sins, because we have Him abiding in our hearts. Our sins
are not merely rolled away for 12 months, they are under the blood.
We are cleansed and forgiven forever when we repent in His name.

Hebrews 10:11-18

> And every priest standeth daily ministering and offering oftentimes
> the same sacrifices, which can never take away sins: but this man,
> after he had offered one sacrifice for sins for ever, sat down on the
> right hand of God; from henceforth expecting till his enemies be made
> his footstool. For by one offering he hath perfected for ever them that
> are sanctified.
>
> Whereof the Holy Ghost also is a witness to us: for after that he
> had said before, This is the covenant that I will make with them after
> those days, saith the Lord, I will put my laws into their hearts, and
> in their minds will I write them; and their sins and iniquities will I
> remember no more. Now where remission of these is, there is no
> more offering for sin.

Forgiven and Forgotten

When God forgives, He forgets. Why? Because when He looks at
the death of His Son Jesus Christ on Calvary, He looks at the most
effective means of abolishing sin there ever was. Therefore, when
we are forgiven, we are forgiven and it is never remembered against
us again.

Hebrews 10:19-31

> Having therefore, brethren, boldness to enter into the holiest by the
> blood of Jesus, by a new and living way, which he hath consecrated
> for us, through the vail, that is to say, his flesh; and having an high
> priest over the house of God; let us draw near with a true heart in
> full assurance of faith, having our hearts sprinkled from an evil

conscience, and our bodies washed with pure water.

Let us hold fast the profession of our faith without wavering; (for he is faithful that promised;) And let us consider one another to provoke unto love and to good works: not forsaking the assembling of ourselves together, as the manner of some is; but exhorting one another: and so much the more, as ye see the day approaching.

For if we sin wilfully after that we have received the knowledge of the truth, there remaineth no more sacrifice for sins, but a certain fearful looking for of judgment and fiery indignation, which shall devour the adversaries. He that despised Moses' law died without mercy under two or three witnesses: of how much sorer punishment, suppose ye, shall he be thought worthy, who hath trodden under foot the Son of God, and hath counted the blood of the covenant, wherewith he was sanctified, an unholy thing, and hath done despite unto the Spirit of grace? For we know him that hath said, Vengeance belongeth unto me, I will recompense, saith the Lord. And again, The Lord shall judge his people. It is a fearful thing to fall into the hands of the living God.

The writer to the Hebrews talks about those who turned away from the law of Moses and were taken outside the camp and stoned. "How much more serious will it be," he says, "if you allow the persecution that is rising against you to cause you to turn your back upon God and your Christian brothers. In effect, you will step upon the Son of God and count His blood of the everlasting covenant as an unholy thing." He also tells them to not strike back at those who are persecuting them, but to leave the vengeance to God, because He says vengeance belongs to Him.

Hebrews 10:32-39

But call to remembrance the former days, in which, after ye were illuminated, ye endured a great fight of afflictions; partly, whilst ye were made a gazingstock both by reproaches and afflictions; and partly, whilst ye became companions of them that were so used. For ye had compassion of me in my bonds, and took joyfully the spoiling of your goods, knowing in yourselves that ye have in heaven a better and an enduring substance.

Cast not away therefore your confidence, which hath great recompence of reward. For ye have need of patience, that, after ye have done the will of God, ye might receive the promise. For yet a little while, and he that shall come will come, and will not tarry. Now the just shall live by faith: but if any man draw back, my soul shall have no pleasure in him. But we are not of them who draw back unto perdition: but of them that believe to the saving of the soul.

The writer is reminding the Hebrew Christians that when they accepted Christ, they did so knowing what the first-generation Christians went through, some of whom were put to death. He says, "You knew you would be facing the same things and you have done a good job. You have endured a great fight. It is as if you have been set on a stage for everyone to look at. Therefore, hold onto your confidence because it has great reward. God will not leave you. He is going to reward you. Do not try to reason it out. Just live by your faith knowing God will take care of you."

Hebrews 11:1-3

Now faith is the substance of things hoped for, the evidence of things not seen. For by it the elders obtained a good report. Through faith we understand that the worlds were framed by the word of God, so that things which are seen were not made of things which do appear.

The writer describes what faith is — the substance of things hoped for. In other words, everything that is hoped for has substance or reality. So the first part of understanding faith is to know that what we hope for is not just a pipe dream or something we imagine. It has reality and substance.

Then, he says faith is not presumption. It is not something we just think is going to be. We have to have evidence. Therefore, faith is strong when it has evidence and not presumption.

Hebrews 11:4-6

By faith Abel offered unto God a more excellent sacrifice than Cain, by which he obtained witness that he was righteous, God testifying of his gifts: and by it he being dead yet speaketh.

By faith Enoch was translated that he should not see death; and was not found, because God had translated him: for before his translation he had this testimony, that he pleased God. But without faith it is impossible to please him: for he that cometh to God must believe that he is, and that he is a rewarder of them that diligently seek him.

The writer tells us that if we want to please God, our starting point is our faith. Notice he says, "For he that cometh to God must believe that he is (that He exists), and that he is a rewarder of them that diligently seek him." This sixth verse is very important to us. First, without faith we cannot please God, but with faith we do please Him. Second, we must believe the fact that God really is. And third, we must believe He is a good God because He rewards. Many Christian people have been led to believe that God is not a good

God — that He does not reward faith. So why do you think God wants us to have faith? Because He wants us to know His existence, His realness, His goodness, and His desire to reward. That is why faith is so important to God and why it should be to us.

Hebrews 11:7-16

> By faith Noah, being warned of God of things not seen as yet, moved with fear, prepared an ark to the saving of his house; by the which he condemned the world, and became heir of the righteousness which is by faith. By faith Abraham, when he was called to go out into a place which he should after receive for an inheritance, obeyed; and he went out, not knowing whither he went. By faith he sojourned in the land of promise, as in a strange country, dwelling in tabernacles with Isaac and Jacob, the heirs with him of the same promise: for he looked for a city which hath foundations, whose builder and maker is God.
>
> Through faith also Sara herself received strength to conceive seed, and was delivered of a child when she was past age, because she judged him faithful who had promised. Therefore sprang there even of one, and him as good as dead, so many as the stars of the sky in multitude, and as the sand which is by the sea shore innumerable.
>
> These all died in faith, not having received the promises, but having seen them afar off, and were persuaded of them, and embraced them, and confessed that they were strangers and pilgrims on the earth. For they that say such things declare plainly that they seek a country. And truly, if they had been mindful of that country from whence they came out, they might have had opportunity to have returned. But now they desire a better country, that is, an heavenly: wherefore God is not ashamed to be called their God: for he hath prepared for them a city.

These people acted upon their faith, for as their faith was released to God it was upon the evidence God would do what He said He would do. And it was upon the fact they did something about it. We cannot just sit in the corner of a room and say, "I have faith — I am going to go out and build something" or "I am going to receive the money I need" or "I am going to be blessed with the Spirit." We cannot just sit there and wait till it happens. Something has to be happening inside our hearts. Then we have to do something about it. And when we do, God will not be ashamed to be called our God.

Hebrews 11:17-22

> By faith Abraham, when he was tried, offered up Isaac: and he that had received the promises offered up his only begotten son, of whom

it was said, That in Isaac shall thy seed be called: accounting that God was able to raise him up, even from the dead; from whence also he received him in a figure.

By faith Isaac blessed Jacob and Esau concerning things to come. By faith Jacob, when he was a dying, blessed both the sons of Joseph; and worshipped, leaning upon the top of his staff.

By faith Joseph, when he died, made mention of the departing of the children of Israel; and gave commandment concerning his bones.

These people believed God in their living and in their dying. They believed Him in their youth, their middle age, and their old age.

Hebrews 11:23-40

By faith Moses, when he was born, was hid three months of his parents, because they saw he was a proper child; and they were not afraid of the king's commandment.

By faith Moses, when he was come to years, refused to be called the son of Pharaoh's daughter; choosing rather to suffer affliction with the people of God, than to enjoy the pleasures of sin for a season; esteeming the reproach of Christ greater riches than the treasures in Egypt: for he had respect unto the recompence of the reward.

By faith he forsook Egypt, not fearing the wrath of the king: for he endured, as seeing him who is invisible. Through faith he kept the passover, and the sprinkling of blood, lest he that destroyed the firstborn should touch them.

By faith they passed through the Red sea as by dry land: which the Egyptians assaying to do were drowned. By faith the walls of Jericho fell down, after they were compassed about seven days. By faith the harlot Rahab perished not with them that believed not, when she had received the spies with peace.

And what shall I more say? for the time would fail me to tell of Gideon, and of Barak, and of Samson, and of Jephthah; of David also, and Samuel, and of the prophets: who through faith subdued kingdoms, wrought righteousness, obtained promises, stopped the mouths of lions, quenched the violence of fire, escaped the edge of the sword, out of weakness were made strong, waxed valiant in fight, turned to flight the armies of the aliens.

Women received their dead raised to life again: and others were tortured, not accepting deliverance; that they might obtain a better resurrection: and others had trial of cruel mockings and scourgings, yea, moreover of bonds and imprisonment: they were stoned, they were sawn asunder, were tempted, were slain with the sword: they wandered about in sheepskins and goatskins; being destitute, afflicted, tormented; (of whom the world was not worthy:) they wandered in

deserts, and in mountains, and in dens and caves of the earth.
And these all, having obtained a good report through faith, received
not the promise: God having provided some better thing for us, that
they without us should not be made perfect.

Faith Regardless of the Outcome

The writer is taking the full sweep of the 2,000 years from Abraham
until the birth of Jesus Christ. He is showing that everything done
was done by faith, not by superior force or superior wisdom. It was
all wrought by faith in God. For example, Shadrach, Meshach, and
Abednego were able to go through the fiery furnace. Elisha escaped
the edge of the sword. Hezekiah came out of weakness and 15 years
were added to his life. The widow of Zarephath received her child
back from the dead through the intervention of Elijah the prophet.
Faith gave remarkable deliverance to these people, for they simply
believed God would do what He said He would do.

Notice that in Verse 36, the tone changes. Others had trials, cruel
mockings, scourgings, bonds, and imprisonment. They were stoned,
sawn asunder, and more. So faith gave remarkable deliverance, but
not always in the same way. This is a very important point. Some
were delivered out of terrible situations. Others went through them.
But faith sustained them in both cases.

You may ask, "Why did some have to go through horrible ordeals
while others did not?" I do not know the answer to that question.
Only God does. All I know is that these people, people just like you
and me, never gave up on their faith. No matter what it was they
faced, whether it was good, bad, or indifferent, they held onto their
faith.

In Verses 39 and 40 we learn that although they held onto their
faith, they did not receive the promise of full blessing from God. It
had to wait until Calvary. And they lived before Calvary. You and I
live after Calvary. So they could not be made complete without us
who live after Calvary and believe through the shed blood of Jesus
Christ by our faith. Together, we make up the whole.

Hebrews 12:1-3

Wherefore seeing we also are compassed about with so great a cloud
of witnesses, let us lay aside every weight, and the sin which doth so
easily beset us, and let us run with patience the race that is set before
us, looking unto Jesus the author and finisher of our faith; who for
the joy that was set before him endured the cross, despising the
shame, and is set down at the right hand of the throne of God. For

consider him that endured such contradiction of sinners against himself, lest ye be wearied and faint in your minds.

As we ended Chapter 11 we saw the great heroes of faith. In Chapter 12 the writer is saying they are now in heaven as a great cloud of witnesses. They are watching us. They are up there rooting for us as we run our race on earth. If we could only hear them with the spiritual ears of faith, we would hear their triumphant voices saying, "You can run the race and you can win it too."

Then he gives the clincher, the absolute way to victory — look to Jesus. Focus on the man who is the originator and completer of our faith. For as we keep our eyes on Jesus, we will win this earthly spiritual race and He will make our faith complete.

Hebrews 12:4-11

Ye have not yet resisted unto blood, striving against sin. And ye have forgotten the exhortation which speaketh unto you as unto children, My son, despise not thou the chastening of the Lord, nor faint when thou art rebuked of him: for whom the Lord loveth he chasteneth, and scourgeth every son whom he receiveth. If ye endure chastening, God dealeth with you as with sons; for what son is he whom the father chasteneth not? But if ye be without chastisement, whereof all are partakers, then are ye bastards, and not sons.

Furthermore we have had fathers of our flesh which corrected us, and we gave them reverence: shall we not much rather be in subjection unto the Father of spirits, and live? For they verily for a few days chastened us after their own pleasure; but he for our profit, that we might be partakers of his holiness.

Now no chastening for the present seemeth to be joyous, but grievous: nevertheless afterward it yieldeth the peaceable fruit of righteousness unto them which are exercised thereby.

Suffering versus Chastisement

The writer makes a distinction between suffering for Christ and being chastised by God for our own shortcomings. Many times we say things we ought not to say, we let bitterness begin to spring up in us, or we are careless with our words. And the Lord begins to chastise us. Why does He chastise us? Because we are children. God chastises us to correct us and bring us into discipline. So the discipline you and I develop as Christians comes first out of what we suffer for Christ. Then it comes out of the chastising we receive from God for our own shortcomings and mistakes.

There are three things I would like to bring to your attention on this. First, we are to bear God's chastising and the suffering that the devil and the world throw against us, because the people of faith who went before us bore theirs. Second, everything you and I suffer is small when compared to what Christ suffered. And three, we bear it because it is sent to discipline us. How important it is that God discipline you and me. For we are certainly not worth much to God, ourselves, or anyone else without discipline.

Hebrews 12:12-29

Wherefore lift up the hands which hang down, and the feeble knees; and make straight paths for your feet, lest that which is lame be turned out of the way; but let it rather be healed.

Follow peace with all men, and holiness, without which no man shall see the Lord: looking diligently lest any man fail of the grace of God; lest any root of bitterness springing up trouble you, and thereby many be defiled; lest there be any fornicator, or profane person, as Esau, who for one morsel of meat sold his birthright. For ye know how that afterward, when he would have inherited the blessing, he was rejected: for he found no place of repentance, though he sought it carefully with tears.

For ye are not come unto the mount that might be touched, and that burned with fire, nor unto blackness, and darkness, and tempest, and the sound of a trumpet, and the voice of words; which voice they that heard entreated that the word should not be spoken to them any more: (for they could not endure that which was commanded, And if so much as a beast touch the mountain, it shall be stoned, or thrust through with a dart: and so terrible was the sight, that Moses said, I exceedingly fear and quake:)

But ye are come unto mount Sion, and unto the city of the living God, the heavenly Jerusalem, and to an innumerable company of angels, to the general assembly and church of the firstborn, which are written in heaven, and to God the Judge of all, and to the spirits of just men made perfect, and to Jesus the mediator of the new covenant, and to the blood of sprinkling, that speaketh better things than that of Abel.

See that ye refuse not him that speaketh. For if they escaped not who refused him that spake on earth, much more shall not we escape, if we turn away from him that speaketh from heaven: whose voice then shook the earth: but now he hath promised, saying, Yet once more I shake not the earth only, but also heaven. And this word, Yet once more, signifieth the removing of those things that are shaken, as of things that are made, that those things which cannot be shaken may remain.

27

Wherefore we receiving a kingdom which cannot be moved, let us have grace, whereby we may serve God acceptably with reverence and godly fear: for our God is a consuming fire.

The writer is taking us back to the time when Moses led the children of Israel out of Egypt. They had never seen the mighty strength of God until then. Abraham, Isaac, Jacob, and Joseph had. But the children of Israel in Egyptian bondage had never really seen the great works of God until Moses and Aaron were able to bring forth the miracles of God that enabled them to escape out of Egypt.

So when they stood before Mount Sinai while Moses was alone with God receiving the Ten Commandments, great fire broke out in the mountain followed by stark darkness. Then storms roared, trumpets blew, words were shouted, and the people below became frightened. Even Moses shook and said, "I fear and my body trembles."

Why did these frightening things happen? First, God chose to get the attention of the people that way. Second, He chose that method to bring them into a reverential awe and fear of Him. God knew that for the children of Israel to make it into the Promised Land, they would have to respect and worship Him as Almighty God.

Hebrews 13:1-8

Let brotherly love continue. Be not forgetful to entertain strangers: for thereby some have entertained angels unawares. Remember them that are in bonds, as bound with them; and them which suffer adversity, as being yourselves also in the body.

Marriage is honourable in all, and the bed undefiled: but whoremongers and adulterers God will judge.

Let your conversation be without covetousness; and be content with such things as ye have: for he hath said, I will never leave thee, nor forsake thee. So that we may boldly say, The Lord is my helper, and I will not fear what man shall do unto me.

Remember them which have the rule over you, who have spoken unto you the word of God: whose faith follow, considering the end of their conversation. Jesus Christ the same yesterday, and to day, and for ever.

Practical Christian Advice

There are seven very practical things the writer says to the Hebrew Christians and to you and me as Christians today. First, let brotherly love continue. Second, be hospitable. Third, have a caring heart. Fourth, hold marriage in the highest position. Fifth, do not be full

of greed. Sixth, hold in high regard and respect those who are over
you in the Lord and in the Church. And seventh, remember the
temporary things of this world will come and go, but Jesus Christ
is the same yesterday, today, and forever.

Hebrews 13:9-19

Be not carried about with divers and strange doctrines. For it is a
good thing that the heart be established with grace; not with meats,
which have not profited them that have been occupied therein. We
have an altar, whereof they have no right to eat which serve the
tabernacle. For the bodies of those beasts, whose blood is brought
into the sanctuary by the high priest for sin, are burned without the
camp.

Wherefore Jesus also, that he might sanctify the people with his
own blood, suffered without the gate. Let us go forth therefore unto
him without the camp, bearing his reproach. For here have we no
continuing city, but we seek one to come.

By him therefore let us offer the sacrifice of praise to God
continually, that is, the fruit of our lips giving thanks to his name.
But to do good and to communicate forget not: for with such sacrifices
God is well pleased.

Obey them that have the rule over you, and submit yourselves: for
they watch for your souls, as they that must give account, that they
may do it with joy, and not with grief: for that is unprofitable for you.

Pray for us: for we trust we have a good conscience, in all things
willing to live honestly. But I beseech you the rather to do this, that
I may be restored to you the sooner.

The writer tells the Hebrew Christians, "Pay no attention to the
Judaizers who are trying to get you to conform to the dietary codes
of the law of Moses, because no food can bring Christ to you." Then
he says, "Forget the sacrifices made with animals because Christ
has become our sacrifice."

Then he sums it up by stating what sacrifice is in the Christian
faith. It is a continual sacrifice of praise to God, the fruit of our lips
giving thanks to His name. And it is putting our faith in action by
helping those in need. God is well pleased with both of these.

Hebrews 13:20-25

Now the God of peace, that brought again from the dead our Lord
Jesus, that great shepherd of the sheep, through the blood of the
everlasting covenant, make you perfect in every good work to do his
will, working in you that which is wellpleasing in his sight, through
Jesus Christ; to whom be glory for ever and ever. Amen.

And I beseech you, brethren, suffer the word of exhortation: for I have written a letter unto you in few words. Know ye that our brother Timothy is set at liberty; with whom, if he come shortly, I will see you. Salute all them that have the rule over you, and all the saints. They of Italy salute you. Grace be with you all. Amen.

The writer makes a very positive statement in his prayer that he believes it is possible for us to be complete in Christ in every good work, to actually do His will, and to please God. Then he says, "Salute all the people of God. Everybody in Italy sends you their best. Our brother Timothy is out of jail and if he gets here in time I will bring him with me when I come to see you." He ends the letter, as so many of the New Testament writers do, with the words, "Grace be with you all. Amen." And may God's grace be with you as we conclude the book written to the Hebrews and go into prayer together.

Heavenly Father, our hearts have been lifted up in faith as we studied the book of Hebrews together. We have felt the passion of Your people. We have experienced their sufferings in our hearts and we have seen how they triumphed in You.

So we receive Your Spirit of triumph today because we are serving a winner, the Lord Jesus Christ. And through Him we are winners. We believe the best is yet to come, through Jesus Christ our Lord. Amen and amen.

The General
Epistle of
James

The General
Epistle of
James

This is the letter of James to the people of God everywhere. We now have Paul's letters behind us and are entering a new phase. It is about 30 years after the death of our Lord. Jesus' half brother, James, is the senior pastor of the church in Jerusalem. He is also the world leader of the new Christian faith.

I want you to keep in mind that James is speaking to you and me as well as to the people of his own day. He talks to us primarily about the trials, tribulations, and temptations we go through as mature Christians. And he certainly knew what it was to face trials and tribulations. Shortly after he wrote this letter, he gave his life as a martyr for the faith at the hands of Herod.

As we study the book of James, we will learn practical ways to acquire the wisdom of God as opposed to the wisdom of this world. We will learn how our faith is to be proved by our works and deeds. James shows us how to develop good relationships with people. He teaches us how to communicate and how to bridle the tongue. And above all, he teaches us that God is our source for healing, health, wholeness, and everything we do.

James 1:1-8

James, a servant of God and of the Lord Jesus Christ, to the twelve tribes which are scattered abroad, greeting.

My brethren, count it all joy when ye fall into divers temptations; knowing this, that the trying of your faith worketh patience. But let patience have her perfect work, that ye may be perfect and entire, wanting nothing.

If any of you lack wisdom, let him ask of God, that giveth to all men liberally, and upbraideth not; and it shall be given him. But let him ask in faith, nothing wavering. For he that wavereth is like a wave

of the sea driven with the wind and tossed. For let not that man think
that he shall receive any thing of the Lord. A double minded man is
unstable in all his ways.

Jesus was a man who lived in the wisdom of God. He never
depended upon the wisdom of this world. That must have made a
powerful impact on James because he says here, "Develop a desire
for the wisdom of God, to the extent that you believe God for it. It
is not going to automatically come your way. You must ask for it
in faith. You put your faith on the wisdom of God that you need.
You are to believe you can live your life in the wisdom of God, in
contrast to depending on the way this world runs its business."
He reminds us that a double-minded person is unstable in all his
ways. In other words, we cannot vacillate by following the wisdom
of God on one occasion and the wisdom of the world on the next
occasion. We cannot go back and forth. This is a rich word to you
and me today because when we face trials, tribulations, and
temptations, we have a way out. We can ask God for the wisest way
to handle it. And God will give us His wisdom.

James 1:9-11

Let the brother of low degree rejoice in that he is exalted: but the
rich, in that he is made low: because as the flower of the grass he
shall pass away. For the sun is no sooner risen with a burning heat,
but it withereth the grass, and the flower thereof falleth, and the grace
of the fashion of it perisheth: so also shall the rich man fade away in
his ways.

Rejoice in Christ, Not Poverty or Wealth

The Romans would often come in and strip some Christians of
all their wealth while they would choose to leave others alone. So
there would frequently be a big division between those Christians
who lost much and those Christians who were allowed to keep what
they gained in worldly goods. James is therefore giving a very
practical word. He is saying, "Do not let the poor person be proud
of his poverty or the rich person be proud of his wealth. For God
is the source of our supply. Therefore, our rejoicing should neither
be in poverty nor in wealth."
Wealth has a deceitfulness that can supplant God as the source
of our lives. We can look to it rather than God. But on the other
hand, those who are without very much can develop a self-pride
about themselves because they do not have much. So, in effect,

James is saying, "The rich Christian should rejoice not in his wealth but in his salvation through Jesus Christ. And the brother or the sister who does not have wealth should rejoice because there is an exaltation through making Christ his source. For Christ his source will supply his needs."

James 1:12-15

> Blessed is the man that endureth temptation: for when he is tried, he shall receive the crown of life, which the Lord hath promised to them that love him.
>
> Let no man say when he is tempted, I am tempted of God: for God cannot be tempted with evil, neither tempteth he any man: but every man is tempted, when he is drawn away of his own lust, and enticed. Then when lust hath conceived, it bringeth forth sin: and sin, when it is finished, bringeth forth death.

James is telling us that God does not hold temptation before us to see how we are going to cope with it. He does not tempt any human being. Rather, our temptations come because of an inner impulse or desire that we nourish and feed. And once we have that desire deep enough inside us, the devil comes and inflames it. He entices us to go ahead and do what we are tempted to do. So when desire reaches a certain point, we yield to temptation and thereby commit sin. Then, if we continue in that sin, James says it brings forth death.

James is saying that if we do not encourage our inner impulses and desires, God will see to it that temptation never takes hold of us. But if we rule God out and follow our own desires, there is nothing God can do. He adds, "Blessed is the man that endureth temptation." He does not mean, "Blessed is the man who is tempted," but "Blessed is the person who endures it because he will receive the crown of life. God is going to reward him." Every temptation you and I overcome carries with it a reward from our heavenly Father.

James 1:16-18

> Do not err, my beloved brethren. Every good gift and every perfect gift is from above, and cometh down from the Father of lights, with whom is no variableness, neither shadow of turning. Of his own will begat he us with the word of truth, that we should be a kind of firstfruits of his creatures.

James is telling us that God did not create us to be sinners or to yield to temptation and sin. For God is good. And not only is He a good God, He is always a good God. He does not change.

James 1:19-27

Wherefore, my beloved brethren, let every man be swift to hear, slow to speak, slow to wrath: for the wrath of man worketh not the righteousness of God. Wherefore lay apart all filthiness and superfluity of naughtiness, and receive with meekness the engrafted word, which is able to save your souls.

But be ye doers of the word, and not hearers only, deceiving your own selves. For if any be a hearer of the word, and not a doer, he is like unto a man beholding his natural face in a glass: for he beholdeth himself, and goeth his way, and straightway forgetteth what manner of man he was. But whoso looketh into the perfect law of liberty, and continueth therein, he being not a forgetful hearer, but a doer of the work, this man shall be blessed in his deed.

If any man among you seem to be religious, and bridleth not his tongue, but deceiveth his own heart, this man's religion is vain. Pure religion and undefiled before God and the Father is this, To visit the fatherless and widows in their affliction, and to keep himself unspotted from the world.

In the age this was written, widows and orphans did not have provision made for them by the government, so they usually became the wards of the church. James is saying, "You see, these fatherless ones and widows in their tribulations, you are to do something about that. You are to make your faith an act of love toward them."

James 2:1-18

My brethren, have not the faith of our Lord Jesus Christ, the Lord of glory, with respect of persons. For if there come unto your assembly a man with a gold ring, in goodly apparel, and there come in also a poor man in vile raiment; and ye have respect to him that weareth the gay clothing, and say unto him, Sit thou here in a good place; and say to the poor, Stand thou there, or sit here under my footstool: are ye not then partial in yourselves, and are become judges of evil thoughts?

Hearken, my beloved brethren, Hath not God chosen the poor of this world rich in faith, and heirs of the kingdom which he hath promised to them that love him? But ye have despised the poor. Do not rich men oppress you, and draw you before the judgment seats? Do not they blaspheme that worthy name by the which ye are called?

If ye fulfil the royal law according to the scripture, Thou shalt love thy neighbour as thyself, ye do well: but if ye have respect to persons, ye commit sin, and are convinced of the law as transgressors. For whosoever shall keep the whole law, and yet offend in one point, he is guilty of all. For he that said, Do not commit adultery, said also, Do not kill. Now if thou commit no adultery, yet if thou kill, thou art become a transgressor of the law.

So speak ye, and so do, as they that shall be judged by the law of liberty. For he shall have judgment without mercy, that hath shewed no mercy; and mercy rejoiceth against judgment.

What doth it profit, my brethren, though a man say he hath faith, and have not works? can faith save him? If a brother or sister be naked, and destitute of daily food, and one of you say unto them, Depart in peace, be ye warmed and filled; notwithstanding ye give them not those things which are needful to the body; what doth it profit? Even so faith, if it hath not works, is dead, being alone. Yea, a man may say, Thou hast faith, and I have works: shew me thy faith without thy works, and I will shew thee my faith by my works.

I do not think James is talking about world hunger, but rather those in the local church who are hungry, do not have proper raiment, housing, or transportation, and people who have really come up against hard times.

James 2:19-26

Thou believest that there is one God; thou doest well: the devils also believe, and tremble. But wilt thou know, O vain man, that faith without works is dead? Was not Abraham our father justified by works, when he had offered Isaac his son upon the altar? Seest thou how faith wrought with his works, and by works was faith made perfect? And the scripture was fulfilled which saith, Abraham believed God, and it was imputed unto him for righteousness: and he was called the Friend of God.

Ye see then how that by works a man is justified, and not by faith only. Likewise also was not Rahab the harlot justified by works, when she had received the messengers, and had sent them out another way? For as the body without the spirit is dead, so faith without works is dead also.

James is saying the Christian experience is not just a head belief. It is a life-style. We cannot earn it, but once we have believed our way into the kingdom of God, our faith is proved in the things we do by our faith. Therefore, our faith and our deeds should be so joined together that they are one. They should never be separate. When we say we believe, that means we go into action.

James 3:1-18

My brethren, be not many masters, knowing that we shall receive the greater condemnation. For in many things we offend all. If any man offend not in word, the same is a perfect man, and able also to bridle the whole body.

Behold, we put bits in the horses' mouths, that they may obey us; and we turn about their whole body. Behold also the ships, which though they be so great, and are driven of fierce winds, yet are they turned about with a very small helm, whithersoever the governor listeth.

Even so the tongue is a little member, and boasteth great things. Behold, how great a matter a little fire kindleth! And the tongue is a fire, a world of iniquity: so is the tongue among our members, that it defileth the whole body, and setteth on fire the course of nature; and it is set on fire of hell.

For every kind of beasts, and of birds, and of serpents, and of things in the sea, is tamed, and hath been tamed of mankind: but the tongue can no man tame; it is an unruly evil, full of deadly poison. Therewith bless we God, even the Father; and therewith curse we men, which are made after the similitude of God. Out of the same mouth proceedeth blessing and cursing. My brethren, these things ought not so to be.

Doth a fountain send forth at the same place sweet water and bitter? Can the fig tree, my brethren, bear olive berries? either a vine, figs? so can no fountain both yield salt water and fresh.

Who is a wise man and endued with knowledge among you? let him shew out of a good conversation his works with meekness of wisdom.

But if ye have bitter envying and strife in your hearts, glory not, and lie not against the truth. This wisdom descendeth not from above, but is earthly, sensual, devilish. For where envying and strife is, there is confusion and every evil work. But the wisdom that is from above is first pure, then peaceable, gentle, and easy to be intreated, full of mercy and good fruits, without partiality, and without hypocrisy. And the fruit of righteousness is sown in peace of them that make peace.

The Christian's Tongue

As Christians, we need not feel that we have to descend to this world's pattern of conversation. We do not have to talk as they talk. You can go almost anywhere and you will hear curse words, erotic words, words of strife, and words that divide people. But, on the other hand, there is a wisdom from above. And when we call upon God for that wisdom, we receive the ability to speak with a pure tongue. In other words, the end result of speaking with the wisdom of God is that we ourselves are easily approached. We are merciful. We are not partial to people. And we are not hypocritical. James is saying the Christian is a person of peace. Therefore, his conversation and his tongue should reflect that.

James 4:1-3

> From whence come wars and fightings among you? come they not hence, even of your lusts that war in your members? Ye lust, and have not: ye kill, and desire to have, and cannot obtain: ye fight and war, yet ye have not, because ye ask not. Ye ask, and receive not, because ye ask amiss, that ye may consume it upon your lusts.

James looks around at the Christians and he sees them fighting with one another, being jealous over what another person has, lusting after possessions, and even wanting to do something violent about it. He says, "You do not have to go through all of that. Remember, you have a source — the Lord Jesus Christ."

James 4:4-10

> Ye adulterers and adulteresses, know ye not that the friendship of the world is enmity with God? whosoever therefore will be a friend of the world is the enemy of God. Do ye think that the scripture saith in vain, The spirit that dwelleth in us lusteth to envy? But he giveth more grace. Wherefore he saith, God resisteth the proud, but giveth grace unto the humble.
>
> Submit yourselves therefore to God. Resist the devil, and he will flee from you. Draw nigh to God, and he will draw nigh to you. Cleanse your hands, ye sinners; and purify your hearts, ye double minded. Be afflicted, and mourn, and weep: let your laughter be turned to mourning, and your joy to heaviness. Humble yourselves in the sight of the Lord, and he shall lift you up.

James is speaking primarily of spiritual adultery. For when we break our intimacy and oneness with God, it is an act of spiritual adultery. We have then taken up a new relationship with this world system and an indirect relationship with the devil himself.

Therefore, we are to resist the devil and the ways of this world, and they will fall off us. But in order to do that, we have to draw nigh to God. Notice that there is a double drawing. We draw ourselves to God and He draws himself to us. The spirit of Christ in us then fights against the things of the world and the things of the devil. He gives us more grace.

James 4:11-17

Speak not evil one of another, brethren. He that speaketh evil of his brother, and judgeth his brother, speaketh evil of the law, and judgeth the law: but if thou judge the law, thou art not a doer of the law, but a judge. There is one lawgiver, who is able to save and to destroy: who art thou that judgest another?

Go to now, ye that say, To day or to morrow we will go into such a city, and continue there a year, and buy and sell, and get gain: whereas ye know not what shall be on the morrow. For what is your life? It is even a vapour, that appeareth for a little time, and then vanisheth away.

For that ye ought to say, If the Lord will, we shall live, and do this, or that. But now ye rejoice in your boastings: all such rejoicing is evil. Therefore to him that knoweth to do good, and doeth it not, to him it is sin.

This was a time when Rome was establishing new colonies and new cities. The Romans would often ask the Jews, especially the merchants, to go to these new areas and set up trading and merchandising. So these people would take a map, look at it, and say, "Where can I make my fortune?" James is saying that a person of God cannot do that. He has to look at God's map. He has to think of God as his source, as the one who decides the course of his life.

James 5:1-6

Go to now, ye rich men, weep and howl for your miseries that shall come upon you. Your riches are corrupted, and your garments are motheaten. Your gold and silver is cankered; and the rust of them shall be a witness against you, and shall eat your flesh as it were fire. Ye have heaped treasure together for the last days.

Behold, the hire of the labourers who have reaped down your fields, which is of you kept back by fraud, crieth: and the cries of them which have reaped are entered into the ears of the Lord of sabaoth. Ye have lived in pleasure on the earth, and been wanton; ye have nourished your hearts, as in a day of slaughter. Ye have condemned and killed the just; and he doth not resist you.

James is not speaking against wealth or riches. In fact, the Bible says, "It is God who giveth thee power to get wealth." But God has always been against the hoarding of riches and resources at the expense of other people. At that point, God stands on the side of the laboring person and shows His concern.

James 5:7-9

> Be patient therefore, brethren, unto the coming of the Lord. Behold,
> the husbandman waiteth for the precious fruit of the earth, and hath
> long patience for it, until he receive the early and latter rain. Be ye
> also patient; stablish your hearts: for the coming of the Lord draweth
> nigh. Grudge not one against another, brethren, lest ye be condemned:
> behold, the judge standeth before the door.

Patience for the Advent of the Lord

James is saying, "Do not get so carried away fighting with one
another over money and position in this world that you lose out on
the greatest thing of all: the coming of the Lord. At the same time,
since you do not know the hour that He is coming, establish yourself
in the Lord. Get a position in Christ that is impregnable so that you
have patience for His advent, His coming."

James 5:10-12

> Take, my brethren, the prophets, who have spoken in the name of
> the Lord, for an example of suffering affliction, and of patience. Behold,
> we count them happy which endure. Ye have heard of the patience
> of Job, and have seen the end of the Lord; that the Lord is very pitiful,
> and of tender mercy.
>
> But above all things, my brethren, swear not, neither by heaven,
> neither by the earth, neither by any other oath: but let your yea be
> yea; and your nay, nay; lest ye fall into condemnation.

James wants to prepare us for the kinds of forces coming against
us that will test our faith as never before, so he calls to the witness
stand the prophets of old who were truly obedient to God in spite
of being mistreated by the world. He also speaks of Job, a righteous
man who in the midst of trials kept his faith.

Then he adds something that is important to us today: the practice
of honesty in speech. In those days, people who made oaths and
included the name of God were more apt to honor them than those
who made oaths without including the name of God. But James is
saying, "When you are called upon as a Christian, just say a simple
yes or a simple no. Do not make a big fancy oath. For you are
responsible to God for what you say. Do not embroider the truth or
maximize the error. Just be straightforward, honest Christian men
and women."

James 5:13-16

Is any among you afflicted? let him pray. Is any merry? let him sing psalms. Is any sick among you? let him call for the elders of the church; and let them pray over him, anointing him with oil in the name of the Lord: and the prayer of faith shall save the sick, and the Lord shall raise him up; and if he have committed sins, they shall be forgiven him.

Confess your faults one to another, and pray one for another, that ye may be healed. The effectual fervent prayer of a righteous man availeth much.

James says the Church is to be a singing church. It is to be a praying church. And it is to be a healing church. The Church is to be a singing, praying, healing group of people.

When he says, "Is any among you afflicted?" James is speaking directly to the exhausted or ill-treated person. And he says, "Pray." In other words, there is a sense of personal responsibility. We are not to sit around and wonder why someone does not pray for us. We are to pray ourselves. And when we are happy, we ourselves are to sing.

Then he asks, "Are there any sick folks among you? Has someone among the people of God fallen with sickness or disease?" If so, that person is to take the initiative and issue a call. He or she is to ask directly for someone to pray healing prayers. They are to call for the elders of the church.

Verse 15 is a very important verse to you and me. The original Greek implies, "The prayer of faith shall save the exhausted one and the Lord shall raise him up." In other words, the Lord shall raise the one up who is exhausted by sins. I want you to notice that first there is a prayer of faith. A prayer of knowing that God is a good God and will save us from our sins, a prayer of faith, must be prayed. Second, the Lord will raise him up and forgive his sins. I have seen that so many times in my healing ministry. When a person is healed, even if he is a sinner, he almost always receives Jesus as his Lord and Savior. There is a double deliverance — one from sickness and another from sin.

Verse 16 says that when we confess our faults one to another, then we are to pray one for another. It is not a matter of merely confessing our trespasses and asking for forgiveness. We are to concentrate on God on behalf of the other person. Notice the emphasis here. We are to do this and as we do, we will be healed. The person who does the praying is himself in a position to be healed.

James 5:17,18

> Elijah was a man subject to like passions as we are, and he prayed earnestly that it might not rain: and it rained not on the earth by the space of three years and six months. And he prayed again, and the heaven gave rain, and the earth brought forth her fruit.

The Power of Prayer

I want you to realize the power of prayer. When we talk about prayer we are not talking about mere words. No, prayer is our inner being set on fire by the desire to reach God. Prayer is a reaching up beyond all the things that are here below. Prayer is crying out in the midst of desperation, lack, want, and hopelessness. Prayer is calling on the one who has never lost a battle, the eternal God. Prayer is reaching up so that God's power may come down to us.

James 5:19,20

> Brethren, if any of you do err from the truth, and one convert him; let him know, that he which converteth the sinner from the error of his way shall save a soul from death, and shall hide a multitude of sins.

James is summing up his book. He is saying, "Men and women of God, if any of you slip away from the Lord or violate some doctrine or truth of the Lord, then the others are to reach out toward you and help bring you back." He is saying, "All that I have taught you in this letter is summed up in this."

Finally, I want to commend to you this precious letter, the book of James, for practical teaching in your daily walk with Jesus.

The First
Epistle General of
Peter

The First
Epistle General of
Peter

As we begin the first epistle of Peter, I want you to keep in mind who Peter was. He was the man who was led to Christ by his brother, Andrew. Jesus saw something very special in Peter because Peter had the stuff of which apostles are made. But he needed the making power of God to bring it out.

Peter had a radical change in his life just prior to the day of Pentecost; on that day he was the first to preach the gospel of Jesus Christ. He was not an educated man, as Paul and the theological leaders of Israel were. But he was an informed person. He grew up in the synagogue school system. Although he did not have university or seminary training, he was highly informed in the Jewish faith.

Peter had the incomparable privilege of walking with Christ three years. He was one of the 12 disciples and was in the inner circle of three men around Christ. He was on the Mount of Transfiguration when the glory of God was revealed in Jesus. He was the man to whom Jesus always paid a lot of attention. And he was the first person to see the empty tomb.

Peter was in Rome when he wrote his first epistle. Nero, the Roman emperor, had already burned Rome and blamed it on the Christians. The most severe persecution the Christians had faced was now taking place. Many were put to death. Others were scattered throughout the world in an effort to save their lives and spread the gospel of Jesus Christ. Peter himself had fled from Nero. It would not be long until he would be caught and crucified in Rome.

I Peter 1:1-3

Peter, an apostle of Jesus Christ, to the strangers scattered throughout

> Pontus, Galatia, Cappadocia, Asia, and Bithynia, elect according to
> the foreknowledge of God the Father, through sanctification of the
> Spirit, unto obedience and sprinkling of the blood of Jesus Christ:
> Grace unto you, and peace, be multiplied.
>
> Blessed be the God and Father of our Lord Jesus Christ, which
> according to his abundant mercy hath begotten us again unto a lively
> hope by the resurrection of Jesus Christ from the dead . . .

Peter begins his letter with his own name, and states that he is
an apostle of Jesus Christ. Then he says his letter is being written
to the strangers who are scattered. These are the Christians who
fled from Rome to Asia Minor.

I Peter 1:4-9

> To an inheritance incorruptible, and undefiled, and that fadeth not
> away, reserved in heaven for you, who are kept by the power of God
> through faith unto salvation ready to be revealed in the last time.
>
> Wherein ye greatly rejoice, though now for a season, if need be, ye
> are in heaviness through manifold temptations: that the trial of your
> faith, being much more precious than of gold that perisheth, though
> it be tried with fire, might be found unto praise and honour and glory
> at the appearing of Jesus Christ: whom having not seen, ye love; in
> whom, though now ye see him not, yet believing, ye rejoice with joy
> unspeakable and full of glory: receiving the end of your faith, even
> the salvation of your souls.

Refined Like Gold

In the fourth verse, Peter says that we who are begotten of God
will receive an inheritance that is absolutely incorruptible, undefiled,
and can never fade away because it is reserved in heaven for us.
We are made citizens of heaven and kept by the power of God
through our faith.

Then he says, "You are rejoicing although the trial of your faith
is going on." Peter realizes the long arm of Rome is reaching to the
ends of the earth wherever the Christians are scattered. Nero is
demanding to be called lord. He has given a law that says whoever
calls Christ Lord is to be killed.

So Peter says, "Listen to me, believers. The trying of your faith is
much more precious than gold when it is tried in the fire." In those

days when gold was refined, the refiner would continue to separate the dross from the gold until he could see his face in the gold. It became like a mirror. So Peter is saying, "The trying of your faith is having the effect that Jesus Christ can see His own face in your life. Therefore, when you find your faith is being tried by the devil, realize it is for the praise and honor of God that He might see His own image in you."

I Peter 1:10-14

Of which salvation the prophets have enquired and searched diligently, who prophesied of the grace that should come unto you: searching what, or what manner of time the Spirit of Christ which was in them did signify, when it testified beforehand the sufferings of Christ, and the glory that should follow. Unto whom it was revealed, that not unto themselves, but unto us they did minister the things, which are now reported unto you by them that have preached the gospel unto you with the Holy Ghost sent down from heaven; which things the angels desire to look into.

Wherefore gird up the loins of your mind, be sober, and hope to the end for the grace that is to be brought unto you at the revelation of Jesus Christ; as obedient children, not fashioning yourselves according to the former lusts in your ignorance: . . .

Peter is saying we should wake up our minds and start realizing the treasure of the gospel we have in us. We are to renew our minds by the Holy Spirit and keep our hope alive because of the second coming. And we are to do it as obedient children rather than trying to fashion ourselves after the ways of the world or the things we used to do before Christ came into our hearts.

I Peter 1:15-25

But as he which hath called you is holy, so be ye holy in all manner of conversation; because it is written, Be ye holy; for I am holy.

And if ye call on the Father, who without respect of persons judgeth according to every man's work, pass the time of your sojourning here in fear: forasmuch as ye know that ye were not redeemed with corruptible things, as silver and gold, from your vain conversation received by traditions from your fathers; but with the precious blood of Christ, as of a lamb without blemish and without spot: who verily was foreordained before the foundation of the world, but was manifest in these last times for you, who by him do believe in God, that raised him up from the dead, and gave him glory; that your faith and hope might be in God.

Seeing ye have purified your souls in obeying the truth through the Spirit unto unfeigned love of the brethren, see that ye love one another with a pure heart fervently: being born again, not of corruptible seed, but of incorruptible, by the word of God, which liveth and abideth for ever.

For all flesh is as grass, and all the glory of man as the flower of grass. The grass withereth, and the flower thereof falleth away: but the word of the Lord endureth for ever. And this is the word which by the gospel is preached unto you.

Peter flatly says we are born again through the Word of God which lives forever. He describes the things of this world as grass in the field which comes up and is withered by the hot sun. In contrast, God's Word is incorruptible and it endures forever.

I Peter 2:1-10

Wherefore laying aside all malice, and all guile, and hypocrisies, and envies, and all evil speakings, as newborn babes, desire the sincere milk of the word, that ye may grow thereby: if so be ye have tasted that the Lord is gracious.

To whom coming, as unto a living stone, disallowed indeed of men, but chosen of God, and precious, ye also, as lively stones, are built up a spiritual house, an holy priesthood, to offer up spiritual sacrifices, acceptable to God by Jesus Christ.

Wherefore also it is contained in the scripture, Behold, I lay in Sion a chief corner stone, elect, precious: and he that believeth on him shall not be confounded. Unto you therefore which believe he is precious: but unto them which be disobedient, the stone which the builders disallowed, the same is made the head of the corner, and a stone of stumbling, and a rock of offence, even to them which stumble at the word, being disobedient: whereunto also they were appointed.

But ye are a chosen generation, a royal priesthood, an holy nation, a peculiar people; that ye should shew forth the praises of him who hath called you out of darkness into marvellous light; which in time past were not a people, but are now the people of God: which had not obtained mercy, but now have obtained mercy.

Peter tells the scattered Christians they are four things: a chosen generation, a royal priesthood, a holy nation, and a peculiar people. All four of these come from the Old Testament. They are the dream of God for His people. As a nation, however, Israel never came to the point of obedience where God could say all these things about her.

But in Jesus Christ we are special. We are a generation of people who are chosen. We are a royal priesthood of believers. We are a group of people who make up a nation among all the nations. We are a holy nation. And we are a peculiar people — not in the sense of being odd, but unique. We are unique and irreplaceable. Why? According to Peter, so that we might show forth the praises of Him who called us out of darkness into His marvelous light.

I Peter 2:11-17

Dearly beloved, I beseech you as strangers and pilgrims, abstain from fleshly lusts, which war against the soul; having your conversation honest among the Gentiles: that, whereas they speak against you as evildoers, they may by your good works, which they shall behold, glorify God in the day of visitation.

Submit yourselves to every ordinance of man for the Lord's sake: whether it be to the king, as supreme; or unto governors, as unto them that are sent by him for the punishment of evildoers, and for the praise of them that do well. For so is the will of God, that with well doing ye may put to silence the ignorance of foolish men: as free, and not using your liberty for a cloak of maliciousness, but as the servants of God. Honour all men. Love the brotherhood. Fear God. Honour the king.

Peter is not praising the dictatorial government of Rome. He is making a point that we are not to use our freedom in Christ, as sojourners passing through this world, to get into conflict or blood battles with the governments of the world.

I Peter 2:18-25

Servants, be subject to your masters with all fear; not only to the good and gentle, but also to the froward. For this is thankworthy, if a man for conscience toward God endure grief, suffering wrongfully. For what glory is it, if, when ye be buffeted for your faults, ye shall take it patiently? but if, when ye do well, and suffer for it, ye take it patiently, this is acceptable with God.

For even hereunto were ye called: because Christ also suffered for us, leaving us an example, that ye should follow his steps: who did no sin, neither was guile found in his mouth: who, when he was reviled, reviled not again; when he suffered, he threatened not; but committed himself to him that judgeth righteously: who his own self bare our sins in his own body on the tree, that we, being dead to sins, should live unto righteousness: by whose stripes ye were healed.

51

For ye were as sheep going astray; but are now returned unto the Shepherd and Bishop of your souls.

Peter is saying that when we suffer, it should be honorable to God. It should not be suffering for our own bad deeds because there is no glory in that from God's standpoint. When we suffer, we are to do it after the example of Jesus who was blameless.

The stripes that Jesus bore have a special significance. For when He took those stripes, He carried within them our sicknesses, our diseases, our wounds, our hurts, our sins, and our needs. Why? So that we might come unto life, be dead to sins, and be healed by His stripes.

I Peter 3:1-7

Likewise, ye wives, be in subjection to your own husbands; that, if any obey not the word, they also may without the word be won by the conversation of the wives; while they behold your chaste conversation coupled with fear. Whose adorning let it not be that outward adorning of plaiting the hair, and of wearing of gold, or of putting on of apparel; but let it be the hidden man of the heart, in that which is not corruptible, even the ornament of a meek and quiet spirit, which is in the sight of God of great price.

For after this manner in the old time the holy women also, who trusted in God, adorned themselves, being in subjection unto their own husbands: even as Sara obeyed Abraham, calling him lord: whose daughters ye are, as long as ye do well, and are not afraid with any amazement.

Likewise, ye husbands, dwell with them according to knowledge, giving honour unto the wife, as unto the weaker vessel, and as being heirs together of the grace of life; that your prayers be not hindered.

The New Testament teaches that the marriage relationship should be like the relationship Christ has with His Church. He loved the Church so much that He gave himself for it. Therefore, the love the husband has for his wife and the wife has for her husband should rise to the heights of giving, submission, respect, and honor. This is something we all have to work at but can achieve as we submit ourselves to Christ.

I Peter 3:8-22

Finally, be ye all of one mind, having compassion one of another, love as brethren, be pitiful, be courteous: Not rendering evil for evil, or railing for railing: but contrariwise blessing; knowing that ye are thereunto called, that ye should inherit a blessing.

For he that will love life, and see good days, let him refrain his tongue from evil, and his lips that they speak no guile: let him eschew evil, and do good; let him seek peace, and ensue it. For the eyes of the Lord are over the righteous, and his ears are open unto their prayers: but the face of the Lord is against them that do evil.

And who is he that will harm you, if ye be followers of that which is good? But and if ye suffer for righteousness' sake, happy are ye: and be not afraid of their terror, neither be troubled; but sanctify the Lord God in your hearts: and be ready always to give an answer to every man that asketh you a reason of the hope that is in you with meekness and fear: having a good conscience; that, whereas they speak evil of you, as of evildoers, they may be ashamed that falsely accuse your good conversation in Christ.

For it is better, if the will of God be so, that ye suffer for well doing, than for evil doing. For Christ also hath once suffered for sins, the just for the unjust, that he might bring us to God, being put to death in the flesh, but quickened by the Spirit: by which also he went and preached unto the spirits in prison; which sometime were disobedient, when once the longsuffering of God waited in the days of Noah, while the ark was a preparing, wherein few, that is, eight souls were saved by water.

The like figure whereunto even baptism doth also now save us (not the putting away of the filth of the flesh, but the answer of a good conscience toward God,) by the resurrection of Jesus Christ: who is gone into heaven, and is on the right hand of God; angels and authorities and powers being made subject unto him

Living in Love

In the third chapter, the apostle is trying to bring us to a decisive point in our relationships so that we will regard one another with honor, respect, and love. It is a point where husbands and wives walk together in the love and understanding of God. And it is where we as Christians are willing to face whatever persecution comes our way, knowing that Christ is our example.

I Peter 4:1-5

Forasmuch then as Christ hath suffered for us in the flesh, arm yourselves likewise with the same mind: for he that hath suffered in the flesh hath ceased from sin; that he no longer should live the rest of his time in the flesh to the lusts of men, but to the will of God.

For the time past of our life may suffice us to have wrought the will of the Gentiles, when we walked in lasciviousness, lusts, excess of wine, revellings, banquetings, and abominable idolatries: wherein they think it strange that ye run not with them to the same excess of riot, speaking evil of you: who shall give account to him that is ready to judge the quick and the dead.

The Romans thought Christians were really out of their minds. For they once had been lustful, drinking, revelling, idolatrous people. But now they refused to live up to the decadent standards the Romans held out for the world. So, the Romans were indignant and struck at the Christians from every side.

I believe this is very appropriate for you and me today. People think we are strange when we do not run around with them and do the things they do. But they do not understand that Christ has changed our lives, that we have a better hope, and that we are going to stand firmly for Christ no matter what the issues are.

I Peter 4:6-11

For this cause was the gospel preached also to them that are dead, that they might be judged according to men in the flesh, but live according to God in the spirit. But the end of all things is at hand: be ye therefore sober, and watch unto prayer. And above all things have fervent charity among yourselves: for charity shall cover the multitude of sins.

Use hospitality one to another without grudging. As every man hath received the gift, even so minister the same one to another, as good stewards of the manifold grace of God. If any man speak, let him speak as the oracles of God; if any man minister, let him do it as of the ability which God giveth: that God in all things may be glorified through Jesus Christ, to whom be praise and dominion for ever and ever. Amen.

Using the Gifts of the Spirit

Peter says that since we have received the charismatic gifts, we should minister with these gifts, not only to the world, but to one another. We should minister to one another with the gifts of the Spirit so that when we speak, we are speaking under the anointing of the Spirit of God. For if we use the ability that God gives us, it is God whose name we are lifting up and praising.

I Peter 4:12-19

Beloved, think it not strange concerning the fiery trial which is to try you, as though some strange thing happened unto you: but rejoice, inasmuch as ye are partakers of Christ's sufferings; that, when his glory shall be revealed, ye may be glad also with exceeding joy. If ye be reproached for the name of Christ, happy are ye; for the spirit of glory and of God resteth upon you: on their part he is evil spoken of, but on your part he is glorified.

But let none of you suffer as a murderer, or as a thief, or as an evildoer, or as a busybody in other men's matters. Yet if any man suffer as a Christian, let him not be ashamed; but let him glorify God on this behalf.

For the time is come that judgment must begin at the house of God: and if it first begin at us, what shall the end be of them that obey not the gospel of God? And if the righteous scarcely be saved, where shall the ungodly and the sinner appear? Wherefore let them that suffer according to the will of God commit the keeping of their souls to him in well doing, as unto a faithful Creator.

Look for the Extra Glory

This is something you and I must learn how to appropriate. For when we are persecuted or put in a bad light for false reasons, there often is an anger that rises up within us, a resentment. We think, "Why has this happened to me? What have I done to deserve it?" The next thing we know, the devil has taken that resentment and caused us to develop animosity, an unforgiving spirit, or bitterness in our hearts.

But Peter is telling us we do not have to live like that. When the false accusations come and the suffering strikes from every side, we can be happy because the glory of God is resting upon us at that moment. Therefore, we are to look for the extra glory when persecution comes against us in this life.

I Peter 5:1-7

The elders which are among you I exhort, who am also an elder, and a witness of the sufferings of Christ, and also a partaker of the glory that shall be revealed: Feed the flock of God which is among you, taking the oversight thereof, not by constraint, but willingly; not for filthy lucre, but of a ready mind; neither as being lords over God's heritage, but being ensamples to the flock. And when the chief

> Shepherd shall appear, ye shall receive a crown of glory that fadeth
> not away.
>   Likewise, ye younger, submit yourselves unto the elder. Yea, all of
> you be subject one to another, and be clothed with humility: for God
> resisteth the proud, and giveth grace to the humble. Humble
> yourselves therefore under the mighty hand of God, that he may exalt
> you in due time: casting all your care upon him; for he careth for you.

Peter is instructing the younger leaders of the church to submit
themselves to the proven older leaders. In addition, all the people
of God are to be subject to one another and be clothed with humility.
Peter remembers that Jesus, his Master, had put on an apron to
wash His disciples' feet. So he is saying that in that spirit we are to
minister to one another. God gives grace to those who will
figuratively wear the apron of humility.

I Peter 5:8-11

> Be sober, be vigilant; because your adversary the devil, as a roaring
> lion, walketh about, seeking whom he may devour: whom resist
> stedfast in the faith, knowing that the same afflictions are
> accomplished in your brethren that are in the world.
>   But the God of all grace, who hath called us unto his eternal glory
> by Christ Jesus, after that ye have suffered a while, make you perfect,
> stablish, strengthen, settle you. To him be glory and dominion for
> ever and ever. Amen.

Peter turns his attention toward the devil. He says the devil is our
adversary and he acts like a roaring lion. I want you to notice he
does not say the devil is a lion. He says he is as a roaring lion.
This may be a reference to Nero's practice of throwing the
Christians to the lions in the Roman Colosseum. Or it may be a
reference to what a pride of lions does when they surround their
prey. The oldest lion, who is toothless and unable to battle, situates
himself in a place where he can be seen. Then he lifts up his head
and roars. So while he attracts attention, the younger lions pounce
upon the innocent prey.
Partner, the devil is roaring to get our attention. But we can rise
up against his roar. He can be resisted. We can resist the devil
because the God of all grace establishes us in maturity and makes
us firmly in His image.

I Peter 5:12-14

> By Silvanus, a faithful brother unto you, as I suppose, I have written

briefly, exhorting, and testifying that this is the true grace of God wherein ye stand. The church that is at Babylon, elected together with you, saluteth you; and so doth Marcus my son. Greet ye one another with a kiss of charity. Peace be with you all that are in Christ Jesus. Amen.

The name Silvanus refers to Silas, who was well known to the Christian churches. He was a tremendous associate of the Apostle Paul for many years but later joined Peter. Silas had a lot to do with the writing of this book. Peter no doubt dictated while Silas took his words down in the Greek language. It was a tremendous help to Peter, so he gave Silas credit in the letter.

Peter concludes his first epistle by telling us to give an affectionate greeting to one another in the agape love of Jesus Christ. This really is a P.S. It is the type of P.S. that Paul uses to end his letters.

The Second
Epistle General of
Peter

The Second
Epistle General of
Peter

II Peter 1:1-11

Simon Peter, a servant and an apostle of Jesus Christ, to them that have obtained like precious faith with us through the righteousness of God and our Saviour Jesus Christ:

Grace and peace be multiplied unto you through the knowledge of God, and of Jesus our Lord, according as his divine power hath given unto us all things that pertain unto life and godliness, through the knowledge of him that hath called us to glory and virtue: whereby are given unto us exceeding great and precious promises: that by these ye might be partakers of the divine nature, having escaped the corruption that is in the world through lust.

And beside this, giving all diligence, add to your faith virtue; and to virtue knowledge; and to knowledge temperance; and to temperance patience; and to patience godliness; and to godliness brotherly kindness; and to brotherly kindness charity.

For if these things be in you, and abound, they make you that ye shall neither be barren nor unfruitful in the knowledge of our Lord Jesus Christ. But he that lacketh these things is blind, and cannot see afar off, and hath forgotten that he was purged from his old sins.

Wherefore the rather, brethren, give diligence to make your calling and election sure: for if ye do these things, ye shall never fall: for so an entrance shall be ministered unto you abundantly into the everlasting kingdom of our Lord and Saviour Jesus Christ.

Peter points out on one hand our finiteness and humanity and on the other hand the eternity of God. Then he speaks of our personal responsibility to add the Christian graces to our lives.

II Peter 1:12-21

> Wherefore I will not be negligent to put you always in remembrance of these things, though ye know them, and be established in the present truth. Yea, I think it meet, as long as I am in this tabernacle, to stir you up by putting you in remembrance; knowing that shortly I must put off this my tabernacle, even as our Lord Jesus Christ hath shewed me.
>
> Moreover I will endeavour that ye may be able after my decease to have these things always in remembrance. For we have not followed cunningly devised fables, when we made known unto you the power and coming of our Lord Jesus Christ, but were eyewitnesses of his majesty. For he received from God the Father honour and glory, when there came such a voice to him from the excellent glory, This is my beloved Son, in whom I am well pleased. And this voice which came from heaven we heard, when we were with him in the holy mount.
>
> We have also a more sure word of prophecy; whereunto ye do well that ye take heed, as unto a light that shineth in a dark place, until the day dawn, and the day star arise in your hearts: knowing this first, that no prophecy of the scripture is of any private interpretation. For the prophecy came not in old time by the will of man: but holy men of God spake as they were moved by the Holy Ghost.

Peter is saying that the Lord has shown him he is going to die. He does not know the day nor the hour, but he knows he will die a martyr's death. He says he has not built his testimony on hearsay or cunningly devised fables, but on Jesus Christ of whom he was an eyewitness.

He even says he was on the Mount of Transfiguration when God spoke to His beloved Son and when the Lord's countenance was altered so that it glowed above the brightness of the sun. He declares, however, that knowing the prophecies of Christ found in the Scriptures is better than hearing the audible witness of God concerning Christ.

II Peter 2:1

> But there were false prophets also among the people, even as there shall be false teachers among you, who privily shall bring in damnable heresies, even denying the Lord that bought them, and bring upon themselves swift destruction.

The apostle Peter says it is inevitable that false prophets will be among God's people. He points out there were false prophets among the people in the days of the Old Testament. Therefore, in the New

Testament age, there will be false teachers who will come in privately, not revealing their real purposes. They will actually deny that Jesus bought them with His shed blood. He is speaking of people who want identification with the Christian Church, but not for the purpose of uplifting the Lord Jesus or preaching the cross and the resurrection. These people are opening themselves up to self-destruction.

II Peter 2:2-11

And many shall follow their pernicious ways; by reason of whom the way of truth shall be evil spoken of. And through covetousness shall they with feigned words make merchandise of you: whose judgment now of a long time lingereth not, and their damnation slumbereth not.

For if God spared not the angels that sinned, but cast them down to hell, and delivered them into chains of darkness, to be reserved unto judgment; and spared not the old world, but saved Noah the eighth person, a preacher of righteousness, bringing in the flood upon the world of the ungodly; and turning the cities of Sodom and Gomorrha into ashes condemned them with an overthrow, making them an ensample unto those that after should live ungodly; and delivered just Lot, vexed with the filthy conversation of the wicked: (For that righteous man dwelling among them, in seeing and hearing, vexed his righteous soul from day to day with their unlawful deeds): the Lord knoweth how to deliver the godly out of temptations, and to reserve the unjust unto the day of judgment to be punished: but chiefly them that walk after the flesh in the lust of uncleanness, and despise government. Presumptuous are they, selfwilled, they are not afraid to speak evil of dignities.

Whereas angels, which are greater in power and might, bring not railing accusation against them before the Lord.

Characteristics of False Teachers

Peter points out four characteristics of false teachers. First, they want personal popularity more than they want to make Jesus popular among the people. Second, they seek personal gain. They want gain for themselves rather than gain for the kingdom of God. Third, they live corrupt lives. They are morally bankrupt and they lead others into immorality. And fourth, they actually lead men further from Christ rather than closer to Him. Peter indicates the danger of these teachers is that they can lead vast numbers of people astray. But their judgment is coming and God will not hold it back.

II Peter 2:12-22

But these, as natural brute beasts, made to be taken and destroyed, speak evil of the things that they understand not; and shall utterly perish in their own corruption; and shall receive the reward of unrighteousness, as they that count it pleasure to riot in the day time. Spots they are and blemishes, sporting themselves with their own deceivings while they feast with you; having eyes full of adultery, and that cannot cease from sin; beguiling unstable souls: an heart they have exercised with covetous practices; cursed children: which have forsaken the right way, and are gone astray, following the way of Balaam the son of Bosor, who loved the wages of unrighteousness; but was rebuked for his iniquity: the dumb ass speaking with man's voice forbad the madness of the prophet.

These are wells without water, clouds that are carried with a tempest: to whom the mist of darkness is reserved for ever. For when they speak great swelling words of vanity, they allure through the lusts of the flesh, through much wantonness, those that were clean escaped from them who live in error. While they promise them liberty, they themselves are the servants of corruption: for of whom a man is overcome, of the same is he brought in bondage.

For if after they have escaped the pollutions of the world through the knowledge of the Lord and Saviour Jesus Christ, they are again entangled therein, and overcome, the latter end is worse with them than the beginning. For it had been better for them not to have known the way of righteousness, than, after they have known it, to turn from the holy commandment delivered unto them. But it is happened unto them according to the true proverb, The dog is turned to his own vomit again; and the sow that was washed to her wallowing in the mire.

This is righteous indignation in action. The apostle Peter is anointed of God and is bearing down on the false teaching the people are getting. He says the false teachers' practices are deceptive, destructive, and finally lead people into apostasy. In fact, it would have been better had the people not even heard the gospel to begin with than to become apostate after knowing Christ. For when a person becomes an apostate, there is no longer a Savior for his soul.

II Peter 3:1-9

This second epistle, beloved, I now write unto you; in both which I stir up your pure minds by way of remembrance: that ye may be mindful of the words which were spoken before by the holy prophets, and of the commandment of us the apostles of the Lord and Saviour: knowing this first, that there shall come in the last days scoffers, walking after their own lusts, and saying, Where is the promise of his coming? for since the fathers fell asleep, all things continue as they were from the beginning of the creation.

For this they willingly are ignorant of, that by the word of God the heavens were of old, and the earth standing out of the water and in the water: whereby the world that then was, being overflowed with water, perished. But the heavens and the earth, which are now, by the same word are kept in store, reserved unto fire against the day of judgment and perdition of ungodly men.

But, beloved, be not ignorant of this one thing, that one day is with the Lord as a thousand years, and a thousand years as one day. The Lord is not slack concerning his promise, as some men count slackness; but is longsuffering to us-ward, not willing that any should perish, but that all should come to repentance.

The false teachers had come in and said, "The prophets told about the coming of the Lord and the apostles told about the second coming. But where is the second coming? He has not come yet. In fact, you said He was going to destroy the world with water and He did. But He will never destroy the world again. Why worry about hell? Why worry about judgment? Why be concerned about the second coming of Christ? That will not happen."

So Peter speaks up and says, "Not so. I want to stir up your pure minds by way of remembrance. When they speak of God destroying the world by water, they have failed to read the rest of the Bible. For God says the next time He destroys the world, it will be by fire. And as surely as He destroyed the old world with the flood, He will destroy this present world with fire from on high."

II Peter 3:10-14

But the day of the Lord will come as a thief in the night; in the which the heavens shall pass away with a great noise, and the elements shall melt with fervent heat, the earth also and the works that are therein shall be burned up.

Seeing then that all these things shall be dissolved, what manner of persons ought ye to be in all holy conversation and godliness, looking for and hasting unto the coming of the day of God, wherein the heavens being on fire shall be dissolved, and the elements shall melt with fervent heat? Nevertheless we, according to his promise, look for new heavens and a new earth, wherein dwelleth righteousness.

Wherefore, beloved, seeing that ye look for such things, be diligent that ye may be found of him in peace, without spot, and blameless.

Peter says we do not know when Christ will return. Therefore, we should live every moment as though He will come right then. But we should also plan our lives ahead as though He will not come in our generation. We should concentrate our thoughts on Christ, on being His witnesses, and on being faithful whether He comes now or in the future.

II Peter 3:15,16

And account that the longsuffering of our Lord is salvation; even as our beloved brother Paul also according to the wisdom given unto him hath written unto you; as also in all his epistles, speaking in them of these things; in which are some things hard to be understood, which they that are unlearned and unstable wrest, as they do also the other scriptures, unto their own destruction.

This is a personal reference to the Apostle Paul. Peter calls him "our beloved brother." He says Paul wrote his letters under the inspiration of the Holy Spirit, just as the other Scriptures were written. He also says there are some things in Paul's inspired writings that are difficult to understand, and people twist them any way they desire. But he adds that people who do so are unstable in their ways and are hastening their own destruction.

II Peter 3:17,18

Ye therefore, beloved, seeing ye know these things before, beware lest ye also, being led away with the error of the wicked, fall from your own stedfastness. But grow in grace, and in the knowledge of our Lord and Saviour Jesus Christ. To him be glory both now and for ever. Amen.

Growing in Grace

As Peter ends his second letter, he says, "Grow in grace." In other words, life is never static. We must go forward or our lives will go backward.

I want to pray with you as we close this great letter. Will you join me in a moment of prayer?

Father, we have read the truths You spoke to the apostle Peter for people of all generations, including us in the now. I pray we will be informed by this book, will study it, and will grow in the grace and knowledge of Christ so we will not be led away into false doctrines. I pray we will be held in the hands of God, ever looking and being prepared for the imminent return of our Savior Jesus Christ.

My dear friend, I pray God will bless you, strengthen you, and cause you to grow in the grace and knowledge of Jesus Christ of Nazareth. Amen and amen.

The First
Epistle General of
John

The First
Epistle General of
John

John was called "John the beloved." He was one of the three
disciples who were especially close to Christ. He wrote the gospel
of John, which presents Jesus Christ as the Son of God. And he wrote
three epistles to people who needed a reminder of who Jesus really
was and is.

As far as we know, when John wrote his three epistles he was in
Ephesus where Paul had established great Christian churches. The
beloved apostle loved the brethren and was very concerned about
them. In his letters, he dealt primarily with three things that were
creeping into the churches. First, a group who denied the divinity
of Jesus Christ was trying to get into the church. Second, others
were teaching that Jesus really was not human. Third, there was a
denial of the union of the two natures, the divine with the human,
in Jesus. Some were teaching that Jesus Christ had not entered into
humanity and become the God-man.

I John 1:1-4

> That which was from the beginning, which we have heard, which we
> have seen with our eyes, which we have looked upon, and our hands
> have handled, of the Word of life; (for the life was manifested, and
> we have seen it, and bear witness, and shew unto you that eternal
> life, which was with the Father, and was manifested unto us;) that
> which we have seen and heard declare we unto you, that ye also may
> have fellowship with us: and truly our fellowship is with the Father,
> and with his Son Jesus Christ. And these things write we unto you,
> that your joy may be full.

John begins by saying that Jesus Christ was from the beginning.
He did not come into existence when He was born of the virgin

71

Mary. No. He existed in eternity past. And He entered into humanity as the touchable, seeable, feelable Son of God.

I John 1:5-10

This then is the message which we have heard of him, and declare unto you, that God is light, and in him is no darkness at all. If we say that we have fellowship with him, and walk in darkness, we lie, and do not the truth: but if we walk in the light, as he is in the light, we have fellowship one with another, and the blood of Jesus Christ his Son cleanseth us from all sin.

If we say that we have no sin, we deceive ourselves, and the truth is not in us. If we confess our sins, he is faithful and just to forgive us our sins, and to cleanse us from all unrighteousness. If we say that we have not sinned, we make him a liar, and his word is not in us.

John tells us that if we say we have never sinned, we are deceiving ourselves and the truth is not in us. In effect, we are saying there was no need for Christ to come, to die on the cross, and to shed His blood. We are saying His blood has no power to cleanse us from sin. We are denying Jesus Christ and impugning the character of God.

On the other hand, if we confess our sins, Jesus Christ is faithful to forgive us and cleanse us not only from the act of sin but from the habit of it as well. We free ourselves to be in right relation with God and allow His cleansing power to operate in our lives.

I John 2:1-6

My little children, these things write I unto you, that ye sin not. And if any man sin, we have an advocate with the Father, Jesus Christ the righteous: and he is the propitiation for our sins: and not for ours only, but also for the sins of the whole world.

And hereby we do know that we know him, if we keep his commandments. He that saith, I know him, and keepeth not his commandments, is a liar, and the truth is not in him. But whoso keepeth his word, in him verily is the love of God perfected: hereby know we that we are in him. He that saith he abideth in him ought himself also so to walk, even as he walked.

Our Advocate

John is saying that when we come to Christ, the bond between us and God is so strong that we have a personal advocate in Jesus Christ who is the propitiation, the satisfaction, for our sins. But not for ours only — the results of Calvary are for the whole world. For whosoever calls upon the Lord can be saved and forgiven.

I John 2:7-11

Brethren, I write no new commandment unto you, but an old commandment which ye had from the beginning. The old commandment is the word which ye have heard from the beginning. Again, a new commandment I write unto you, which thing is true in him and in you: because the darkness is past, and the true light now shineth.

He that saith he is in the light, and hateth his brother, is in darkness even until now. He that loveth his brother abideth in the light, and there is none occasion of stumbling in him. But he that hateth his brother is in darkness, and walketh in darkness, and knoweth not whither he goeth, because that darkness hath blinded his eyes.

John is saying, "It is easy to say, 'I am a Christian and I am walking in the light.' But if you hate your brother you are in darkness, because he that loves his brother abides in light."

John connects love with light. In other words, if we do not love people, we see everything wrong in their lives. Everything wrong becomes magnified. But if we see with the light of love, their faults are not nearly as great because we truly love them as brothers or sisters in Christ.

I John 2:12-17

I write unto you, little children, because your sins are forgiven you for his name's sake. I write unto you, fathers, because ye have known him that is from the beginning. I write unto you, young men, because ye have overcome the wicked one. I write unto you, little children, because ye have known the Father. I have written unto you, fathers, because ye have known him that is from the beginning. I have written unto you, young men, because ye are strong, and the word of God abideth in you, and ye have overcome the wicked one.

Love not the world, neither the things that are in the world. If any man love the world, the love of the Father is not in him. For all that is in the world, the lust of the flesh, and the lust of the eyes, and the pride of life, is not of the Father, but is of the world. And the world passeth away, and the lust thereof: but he that doeth the will of God abideth for ever.

I believe John is making a great distinction between loving the world as people and loving the world as a thing. We are to love the people of the world. But we are not to love the things that motivate the world to be the world that it is. We are not to love the practice of sin.

I John 2:18-26

Little children, it is the last time: and as ye have heard that antichrist shall come, even now are there many antichrists; whereby we know that it is the last time. They went out from us, but they were not of us: for if they had been of us, they would no doubt have continued with us: but they went out, that they might be made manifest that they were not all of us.

But ye have an unction from the Holy One, and ye know all things. I have not written unto you because ye know not the truth, but because ye know it, and that no lie is of the truth. Who is a liar but he that denieth that Jesus is the Christ? He is antichrist, that denieth the Father and the Son. Whosoever denieth the Son, the same hath not the Father: [but] he that acknowledgeth the Son hath the Father also.

Let that therefore abide in you, which ye have heard from the beginning. If that which ye have heard from the beginning shall remain in you, ye also shall continue in the Son, and in the Father. And this is the promise that he hath promised us, even eternal life.

These things have I written unto you concerning them that seduce you.

John is saying, "The spirit of Antichrist is already here because many people have come into your company pretending to be Christians and then left because they thought they did not need to believe in the divinity of Christ." He adds, "I do not want you to pay any attention to them, because if they were of us, they would not have left us."

I John 2:27-29

But the anointing which ye have received of him abideth in you, and ye need not that any man teach you: but as the same anointing teacheth you of all things, and is truth, and is no lie, and even as it hath taught you, ye shall abide in him.

And now, little children, abide in him; that, when he shall appear, we may have confidence, and not be ashamed before him at his coming. If ye know that he is righteous, ye know that every one that doeth righteousness is born of him.

When John says in Verse 27, "But the anointing which ye have received of him abideth in you," he is dealing with the gift of the

Holy Spirit. He is saying, "When the Spirit of God abides in you, you can detect the false teachers. You will know them as liars because the Holy Spirit will reveal them to you." He also says, "Be sure you abide in Christ so you will not be caught unprepared at His second coming."

I John 3:1-8

Behold, what manner of love the Father hath bestowed upon us, that we should be called the sons of God: therefore the world knoweth us not, because it knew him not. Beloved, now are we the sons of God, and it doth not yet appear what we shall be: but we know that, when he shall appear, we shall be like him; for we shall see him as he is. And every man that hath this hope in him purifieth himself, even as he is pure.

Whosoever committeth sin transgresseth also the law: for sin is the transgression of the law. And ye know that he was manifested to take away our sins; and in him is no sin. Whosoever abideth in him sinneth not: whosoever sinneth hath not seen him, neither known him.

Little children, let no man deceive you: he that doeth righteousness is righteous, even as he is righteous. He that committeth sin is of the devil; for the devil sinneth from the beginning. For this purpose the Son of God was manifested, that he might destroy the works of the devil.

Straight Line to God

Many years ago the Lord gave me the phrase, "straight line to God." In other words, if you are not on the straight line to God, you are on the devil's line. For sin is a straight line to the devil.

John points out that sin originated with the devil. He was the first sinner, the first to rebel against God. He sinned and began to take over God's world. Therefore, God sent His Son to destroy the devil's works and regain the title, or deed to the earth. And that He did.

I want to stop and pray with you.

Father, You sent Your Son Jesus Christ into this world. You manifested Him that He might destroy the works of the devil. I thank You for that. And I pray for this my partner.

Dear partner, I pray that Jesus Christ of Nazareth will rise up within you in new power. I pray you will release your faith and begin to say, "Jesus, I believe You are delivering me. I believe You are freeing me from the works of the devil. I receive deliverance from the power of the enemy to destroy me. I receive the life of God in my being. And I receive it through Jesus Christ of Nazareth." Amen and amen.

I John 3:9

> Whosoever is born of God doth not commit sin; for his seed remaineth in him: and he cannot sin, because he is born of God.

John is talking about the Word of God as God's seed in believers. Because the Word of God is in us and we are in the Word of God, we do not have the desire to sin. He is not talking about an occasional stumbling, for we all need to be cleansed from time to time. He is talking about knowing who we are in Christ to the extent that we want to have nothing to do with sin because it defiles our lives.

I John 3:10-16

> In this the children of God are manifest, and the children of the devil: whosoever doeth not righteousness is not of God, neither he that loveth not his brother. For this is the message that ye heard from the beginning, that we should love one another. Not as Cain, who was of that wicked one, and slew his brother. And wherefore slew he him? Because his own works were evil, and his brother's righteous. Marvel not, my brethren, if the world hate you.
>
> We know that we have passed from death unto life, because we love the brethren. He that loveth not his brother abideth in death. Whosoever hateth his brother is a murderer: and ye know that no murderer hath eternal life abiding in him. Hereby perceive we the love of God, because he laid down his life for us: and we ought to lay down our lives for the brethren.

John says we should be willing to lay down our lives for the brethren. In other words, we believers must be so full of the love of God that we are ready to lay down our lives for one another. How can we do that? First, we can do it by not believing everything we hear or read about our brothers and sisters in the Lord. We can wait until the facts are in. Second, we can pray for one another rather than gossiping or accusing. And third, when necessary we can stand up for fellow Christians when they are falsely accused.

I John 3:17-24

> But whoso hath this world's good, and seeth his brother have need, and shutteth up his bowels of compassion from him, how dwelleth the love of God in him? My little children, let us not love in word,

neither in tongue; but in deed and in truth. And hereby we know that we are of the truth, and shall assure our hearts before him.

For if our heart condemn us, God is greater than our heart, and knoweth all things. Beloved, if our heart condemn us not, then have we confidence toward God. And whatsoever we ask, we receive of him, because we keep his commandments, and do those things that are pleasing in his sight.

And this is his commandment, That we should believe on the name of his Son Jesus Christ, and love one another, as he gave us commandment. And he that keepeth his commandments dwelleth in him, and he in him. And hereby we know that he abideth in us, by the Spirit which he hath given us.

Pleasing God

John says that whatsoever we ask, we will receive from God if we keep His commandments and do the things that are pleasing in His sight. In other words, doing the things that please God involves more than just keeping His commandments. For if we keep His commandments in the way He meant for us to, it will be a great pleasure. We will love to do them. And when we do them, we can expect to receive from God.

I John 4:1-4

Beloved, believe not every spirit, but try the spirits whether they are of God: because many false prophets are gone out into the world. Hereby know ye the Spirit of God: Every spirit that confesseth that Jesus Christ is come in the flesh is of God: and every spirit that confesseth not that Jesus Christ is come in the flesh is not of God: and this is that spirit of antichrist, whereof ye have heard that it should come; and even now already is it in the world.

Ye are of God, little children, and have overcome them: because greater is he that is in you, than he that is in the world.

John declares that every person has a spirit. We either have the Spirit of God or we have the spirit of the devil. Therefore, every person who works among the children of God must be tested to see if he is of God or of the devil. The Spirit that is of God confesses that Jesus Christ came in the flesh. But spirits not of God deny that Jesus Christ came in the flesh. They declare He did not come into the world as the Son of God. They say He did not go to the cross and die for our sins. They say there is no such thing as salvation, a new birth, or becoming new creatures in Jesus Christ.

In fact, John says they have the spirit of Antichrist. He says, "I want you to know that the spirit of Antichrist is already in the world. You must be alert and sensitive to the fact that the devil is among you to discredit the Lord Jesus Christ. But remember, you are of God and you have the power to overcome, because greater is He that is in you than he that is in the world."

John is saying, "You can test the spirits. You can overcome them because there is someone in you that is greater than the devil, greater than the evil spirits, and greater than the spirit of the world. He is Jesus Christ of Nazareth who came in the flesh."

I John 4:5-12

They are of the world: therefore speak they of the world, and the world heareth them. We are of God: he that knoweth God heareth us; he that is not of God heareth not us. Hereby know we the spirit of truth, and the spirit of error.

Beloved, let us love one another: for love is of God; and every one that loveth is born of God, and knoweth God. He that loveth not knoweth not God; for God is love. In this was manifested the love of God toward us, because that God sent his only begotten Son into the world, that we might live through him. Herein is love, not that we loved God, but that he loved us, and sent his Son to be the propitiation for our sins.

Beloved, if God so loved us, we ought also to love one another. No man hath seen God at any time. If we love one another, God dwelleth in us, and his love is perfected in us.

The Source of Love

Who is the source of love? It is not the devil. Nor is it the world. It is God. John tells us that God is love. But God is greater than love. For His love is manifested toward us in the form of His own Son begotten into the world. The sending of Jesus is the love of God in action.

His love also is the satisfaction for our sins. Why? Because the cross is more than a bloody crucifix. It is the propitiation for our sins through the person of Jesus Christ. It is love that we can see, feel, and know.

Therefore, because God loves us, we ought to love one another. For when we do, we show the family likeness. Others can see God when they see His children loving one another. Love causes people to say, "That person lets me know there is a God. And He is a God of love."

I John 4:13-21

Hereby know we that we dwell in him, and he in us, because he hath given us of his Spirit. And we have seen and do testify that the Father sent the Son to be the Saviour of the world. Whosoever shall confess that Jesus is the Son of God, God dwelleth in him, and he in God.

And we have known and believed the love that God hath to us. God is love; and he that dwelleth in love dwelleth in God, and God in him. Herein is our love made perfect, that we may have boldness in the day of judgment: because as he is, so are we in this world.

There is no fear in love; but perfect love casteth out fear; because fear hath torment. He that feareth is not made perfect in love. We love him, because he first loved us.

If a man say, I love God, and hateth his brother, he is a liar: for he that loveth not his brother whom he hath seen, how can he love God whom he hath not seen? And this commandment have we from him, That he who loveth God love his brother also.

When I think about God, I think about love. God is love. That is why He gave Jesus Christ, His only begotten Son, to die for our sins. He loves you and me.

In fact, God loves us first. He loves everybody before they love Him. And He even loves those who do not love Him. Therefore, when we have God who is love, we love others. And if we say we are of God but do not love others, we really are liars. Love is the surest sign that God is in our lives.

I John 5:1-5

Whosoever believeth that Jesus is the Christ is born of God: and every one that loveth him that begat loveth him also that is begotten of him.

By this we know that we love the children of God, when we love God, and keep his commandments. For this is the love of God, that we keep his commandments: and his commandments are not grievous. For whatsoever is born of God overcometh the world: and this is the victory that overcometh the world, even our faith. Who is he that overcometh the world, but he that believeth that Jesus is the Son of God?

John begins the fifth chapter with the word "whosoever." He says, "Whosoever believeth that Jesus is the Christ is born of God." John does not use that term loosely, for a Christian is one who uses his faith to believe that Jesus is the real Christ. And in that belief, a birth happens. A new creation emerges. Another child is born into the kingdom of God.

I John 5:6-8

> This is he that came by water and blood, even Jesus Christ; not by water only, but by water and blood. And it is the Spirit that beareth witness, because the Spirit is truth.
>
> For there are three that bear record in heaven, the Father, the Word, and the Holy Ghost: and these three are one. And there are three that bear witness in earth, the spirit, and the water, and the blood: and these three agree in one.

John gives a tremendous truth about the way Jesus Christ came to be the Savior of the world. He says Jesus came by water, that is, by baptism, through John the Baptist. And He came by giving His blood on Calvary as a sacrifice for our sins.

I John 5:9-15

> If we receive the witness of men, the witness of God is greater: for this is the witness of God which he hath testified of his Son. He that believeth on the Son of God hath the witness in himself: he that believeth not God hath made him a liar; because he believeth not the record that God gave of his Son. And this is the record, that God hath given to us eternal life, and this life is in his Son. He that hath the Son hath life: and he that hath not the Son of God hath not life.
>
> These things have I written unto you that believe on the name of the Son of God; that ye may know that ye have eternal life, and that ye may believe on the name of the Son of God.
>
> And this is the confidence that we have in him, that, if we ask any thing according to his will, he heareth us: and if we know that he hear us, whatsoever we ask, we know that we have the petitions that we desired of him.

John says we should pray according to the will of God. So, how are we to pray in God's will? First, we pray on the basis of God in us. Second, we pray on the basis of the Word of God that we study and learn by the Spirit. And third, we pray on the basis of the life of Christ that we see in the Bible. When we do these three things, we will pray according to the will of God.

I John 5:16,17

> If any man see his brother sin a sin which is not unto death, he shall ask, and he shall give him life for them that sin not unto death. There is a sin unto death: I do not say that he shall pray for it. All unrighteousness is sin: and there is a sin not unto death.

Christian Intercession

John is saying we have an intercessory role as brothers in Christ to pray for one another when one of us commits a sin not unto death, that is, when we have not denied that Jesus is the Christ. Christians who have not rejected Jesus Christ as the Son of God can be forgiven and restored. And it is within our work as believers to undergo intercessory prayer for them.

I John 5:18-21

> We know that whosoever is born of God sinneth not; but he that is begotten of God keepeth himself, and that wicked one toucheth him not. And we know that we are of God, and the whole world lieth in wickedness.
>
> And we know that the Son of God is come, and hath given us an understanding, that we may know him that is true, and we are in him that is true, even in his Son Jesus Christ. This is the true God, and eternal life. Little children, keep yourselves from idols. Amen.

John says when we are born of God, we are no longer habitual sinners. We do not continue in sin because we know we are born again.

Then he says, "That wicked one toucheth him not." What John is referring to is the fact that the devil cannot touch our faith in Jesus Christ as the Son of God. It is true the devil can touch our circumstances and our flesh. But he cannot get inside us to touch the connection we have with Jesus Christ, the Son of God and our personal Savior. What a powerful, victorious way to close the first epistle of John the apostle.

The Second
Epistle of
John

The Second
Epistle of
John

As we begin the second epistle, or letter, of John, I want you to keep in mind the three things that stand out in this epistle: the command to walk in the truth of God, the command to love one another, and the command to not accept false teachers.

II John 1-4

> The elder unto the elect lady and her children, whom I love in the truth; and not I only, but also all they that have known the truth; for the truth's sake, which dwelleth in us, and shall be with us for ever. Grace be with you, mercy, and peace, from God the Father, and from the Lord Jesus Christ, the Son of the Father, in truth and love.
> I rejoiced greatly that I found of thy children walking in truth, as we have received a commandment from the Father.

John is writing to a group of people in a local congregation. He says he is the elder. In other words, he is the aged one. In fact, he is the last living apostle of the original twelve.

He calls this church the elect lady. This must be a very special name he had for this particular congregation. He tells them he loves them in the truth. Then he says, "I rejoiced greatly that I found your children walking in truth." John's statement tells us first of all that he had been with them and had personally observed their walk in the truth. Then it tells us that he knew the absolute value of walking in the truth.

II John 5,6

> And now I beseech thee, lady, not as though I wrote a new commandment unto thee, but that which we had from the beginning, that we love one another. And this is love, that we walk after his

85

commandments. This is the commandment, That, as ye have heard from the beginning, ye should walk in it.

The Love Commandment

John is referring to the agape kind of love, the deepest form of love we express one toward another as members of the Body of Christ. He says that just as truth is a commandment of God, so love is a commandment of God. It is an act. Love is something we do regardless of the apparent value of the person or how we feel.

II John 7-11

For many deceivers are entered into the world, who confess not that Jesus Christ is come in the flesh. This is a deceiver and an antichrist.

Look to yourselves, that we lose not those things which we have wrought, but that we receive a full reward. Whosoever transgresseth, and abideth not in the doctrine of Christ, hath not God. He that abideth in the doctrine of Christ, he hath both the Father and the Son.

If there come any unto you, and bring not this doctrine, receive him not into your house, neither bid him God speed: for he that biddeth him God speed is partaker of his evil deeds.

Stand Up for the Real Jesus

How can we apply this today? First, we must be aware there are many teachers who deny that Jesus Christ has come in the flesh. There are even so-called preachers who deny the divinity of Jesus. They say He is a good man or a prophet. But they deny He is the Son of God. I want you to know that if we buy their teaching, we will lose our hope of salvation. For it is only through Jesus that we come to God. Peter says, "There is none other name given among men whereby we must be saved except the name of Jesus."

Second, we must see to it that deceivers have no part in our congregations, in our homes, or with our children. We must stand up for the Lord Jesus Christ. We must not let those who deny the incarnation of Jesus control the Body of Christ on earth.

II John 12,13

Having many things to write unto you, I would not write with paper and ink: but I trust to come unto you, and speak face to face, that our joy may be full. The children of thy elect sister greet thee. Amen.

In my own view, the face-to-face meeting has no substitute. There is nothing that can take the place of going out among people and preaching, teaching, and praying for their deliverance. I think I have some of the same feelings that John had when he wrote this letter.

The second letter of John is very brief, but it is very necessary. I end it by reminding you: Walk in the truth of God, let your love flow out of your heart, but do not get mixed up with people who deny our Lord Jesus Christ and His shed blood.

The Third
Epistle of
John

The Third
Epistle of
John

We come to the magnificent little book of III John. I love this little book. It only has one chapter, but it has profoundly changed my life.

III John 1-8

The elder unto the wellbeloved Gaius, whom I love in the truth.

Beloved, I wish above all things that thou mayest prosper and be in health, even as thy soul prospereth. For I rejoiced greatly, when the brethren came and testified of the truth that is in thee, even as thou walkest in the truth. I have no greater joy than to hear that my children walk in truth.

Beloved, thou doest faithfully whatsoever thou doest to the brethren, and to strangers; which have borne witness of thy charity before the church: whom if thou bring forward on their journey after a godly sort, thou shalt do well: because that for his name's sake they went forth, taking nothing of the Gentiles. We therefore ought to receive such, that we might be fellowhelpers to the truth.

My Discovery of III John 2

John says these immortal words: "Beloved, I wish above all things that thou mayest prosper and be in health, even as thy soul prospereth."

The word "health" is used in this verse to mean both health and soundness. And the word "prosperity" refers to success. It goes all the way back to God's creative process when He made man to be prosperous and successful. The same term is specifically used by Moses and Joshua. John is saying, "Gaius, your soul is doing well in a spiritual way. So, I pray that your bodily health and your financial prosperity will do equally well."

In 1947, as a college student and young preacher, I providentially discovered III John 2. And it changed my life. Evelyn, my two children, and I desperately needed to know that God is good. Yes, I knew in many ways that God is good. He had saved me. He had healed me from tuberculosis. He had led my life in many ways. But somehow it failed to register in me that God is truly good.

I remember how I read this verse to Evelyn, and then she and I read it together. We began to rejoice. I said for the first time in my life, "God is a good God. God is a good God." I was inspired. Evelyn was inspired. I did not go to the university that day. Evelyn and I spent most of the day just studying this scripture and others like it. We took our concordance and went through the Bible to discover the verses that spoke of the goodness of God.

Many days later I came into the realization of the eternal truth of God that He wishes above all things for His children to have health and prosperity that is equal to that of their souls. So I began to preach a fresh, new message that God is good and God loves you. And I began to pray for the people. There was a lot of opposition from every side. Some said I was not preaching the truth of the Bible. But I just stood up and read that scripture over and over. I went to other scriptures and read them too. And I showed how throughout the Bible, God wanted to bless His people spiritually, physically, and financially.

The flame was in my heart. I was anointed of God to preach, pray, and bring deliverance to people. This healing ministry got under way and like a prairie fire swept across America and into more than 40 nations on all continents. And today, I am as inspired with this as I was the first moment I read, "Beloved, I wish above all things that thou mayest prosper and be in health, even as thy soul prospereth."

III John 9-14

I wrote unto the church: but Diotrephes, who loveth to have the preeminence among them, receiveth us not. Wherefore, if I come, I will remember his deeds which he doeth, prating against us with malicious words: and not content therewith, neither doth he himself receive the brethren, and forbiddeth them that would, and casteth them out of the church.

Beloved, follow not that which is evil, but that which is good. He that doeth good is of God: but he that doeth evil hath not seen God. Demetrius hath good report of all men, and of the truth itself; yea, and we also bear record; and ye know that our record is true.

I had many things to write, but I will not with ink and pen write unto thee: But I trust I shall shortly see thee, and we shall speak face to face. Peace be to thee. Our friends salute thee. Greet the friends by name.

Knowing the Goodness of God

John says, "Beloved Gaius, follow that which is good." John talks a lot about the goodness of God. To him God is good. For when he walked with Jesus the three years the Lord was on the earth, he saw what the heavenly Father is like. Jesus said to the disciples one time, "If you have seen Me, you have seen the Father because the Father is just like I am. And I am just like My Father is."

John closes his little letter by recommending a brother to Gaius. He has just mentioned Diotrephes as a dictatorial type who really does not fit in the kingdom of God. But there is a traveling minister, Demetrius, who is coming to the church where Gaius is that John personally recommends. He says Demetrius has a good report of all men. He is pointing out that Gaius should receive the minister and see to it that the church receives him too.

I want to pray with you as we close the third letter of John.

Our heavenly Father, we feel the uplifting power of Your Son Jesus Christ. The Holy Spirit is welling up within us. We feel like shouting the victory and letting everybody know that You are a good God, You love us, You care for us, and You are closer to us than our breath.

Dear friend, I pray that Jesus and His goodness will just explode in your being. I pray you will open your mind to His goodness. May you learn more and more how good He is and how you can love and serve Him all the days of your life with gladness and joy. Amen and amen.

The General
Epistle of
Jude

The General
Epistle of
Jude

We believe that Jude was the half brother of Jesus. In other words, Mary was the mother of both Jesus and Jude, while Joseph was the father of Jude and God was the Father of Jesus. In Mark 6:3 we read, "Is not this the carpenter, the son of Mary, the brother of James, and Joses, and of Juda (Jude), and Simon?" Matthew 13:55 also places Jude among the brothers of Jesus.

The Bible indicates that at one time the family of Jesus did not understand His mission. However, the impression Jesus made on His family must have become very great. For Jude finally received the Lord Jesus Christ as his own personal Savior and became active in the church. He later was so moved by compassion that under the inspiration of the Holy Spirit, he wrote this wonderful epistle.

The book of Jude hits like a hammer blow. The author urges us to stand up for the faith. He is writing during a time when the devil is raging against the Church with renewed vigor. Evil people have infiltrated the Church and are creating disorder among the people of God. And yet, the work of God is spreading throughout the world. The Christian faith has taken deep root in the lives of thousands of people, and many churches are springing up. Thus, the epistle of Jude was not only relevant for the Christians of Jude's day, it is appropriate for us today. It speaks directly to you and me in the now.

Jude 1-3

Jude, the servant of Jesus Christ, and brother of James, to them that are sanctified by God the Father, and preserved in Jesus Christ, and called. Mercy unto you, and peace, and love, be multiplied.

Beloved, when I gave all diligence to write unto you of the common salvation, it was needful for me to write unto you, and exhort you

that ye should earnestly contend for the faith which was once
delivered unto the saints.

Jude indicates he is a servant of Jesus Christ. He is writing to
Christian people who are sanctified and are set apart to serve God,
are called of God into the uniqueness of Jesus Christ the Son of God,
are beloved, have a common salvation, and are defending the faith
of Jesus Christ.

Jude 4-7

For there are certain men crept in unawares, who were before of old
ordained to this condemnation, ungodly men, turning the grace of
our God into lasciviousness, and denying the only Lord God, and our
Lord Jesus Christ.
I will therefore put you in remembrance, though ye once knew this,
how that the Lord, having saved the people out of the land of Egypt,
afterward destroyed them that believed not. And the angels which
kept not their first estate, but left their own habitation, he hath
reserved in everlasting chains under darkness unto the judgment of
the great day.
Even as Sodom and Gomorrha, and the cities about them in like
manner, giving themselves over to fornication, and going after strange
flesh, are set forth for an example, suffering the vengeance of eternal
fire.

A Reminder of God's Judgments

Jude states that ungodly men have come into the Body of Christ.
They are motivated by Satan himself. They are exchanging the grace
of God for blatant immorality and denying the Lord Jesus Christ.
These men are subtly turning the attention of the Christians away
from the moral and spiritual order of God.
So Jude says, "I want to bring to your remembrance three terrible
events from the past that serve as divine warnings." Then he reminds
them of the fate of the Israelites due to their unbelief. He reminds
them of the angels' rebellion against God and their eternal
punishment in darkness. And he reminds them of how God took
vengeance upon Sodom and Gomorrah because of their terrible
immorality.
My friend, it is very important that we go back and read these
three terrible incidents in history and let them be a warning to us.
For if God did not spare the Israelites, if He did not spare the angels,
and if He did not spare Sodom and Gomorrah, how can we think we

are going to escape if we get into unbelief which leads to all kinds of sins? If God kept His word then, He will keep it now.

Jude 8,9

> Likewise also these filthy dreamers defile the flesh, despise dominion, and speak evil of dignities. Yet Michael the archangel, when contending with the devil he disputed about the body of Moses, durst not bring against him a railing accusation, but said, The Lord rebuke thee.

Jude then gives the illustration of how Michael the archangel contended with the devil over the body of Moses. He points out that when Michael denied the devil authority over the body of Moses, he did not bring an accusation against him but said, "The Lord rebuke thee." He was very careful not to speak evil even of the fallen angels.

When we as Christians rebuke the devil, we do not rebuke him in our power. None of us are a match for the devil or a demon. We have to have the power greater than ourselves — the name of Jesus. We say, "In the name of Jesus, we rebuke you, Satan. We resist you. And we command you to leave us."

Jude 10,11

> But these speak evil of those things which they know not: but what they know naturally, as brute beasts, in those things they corrupt themselves. Woe unto them! for they have gone in the way of Cain, and ran greedily after the error of Balaam for reward, and perished in the gainsaying of Core.

Three More Examples

Jude points out three additional tragic examples. One is Cain, the first-born son of Adam and Eve who got out of his created order and murdered his brother. He was a man who rejected everything that was spiritual. The second is Balaam, who attempted to put a curse on the children of Israel for financial gain. And the third is Core, who rejected the God-ordained leadership of Moses and was swallowed up by an earthquake.

Jude 12-19

> These are spots in your feasts of charity, when they feast with you, feeding themselves without fear: clouds they are without water, carried about of winds; trees whose fruit withereth, without fruit,

twice dead, plucked up by the roots; raging waves of the sea, foaming out their own shame; wandering stars, to whom is reserved the blackness of darkness for ever.

And Enoch also, the seventh from Adam, prophesied of these, saying, Behold, the Lord cometh with ten thousands of his saints, to execute judgment upon all, and to convince all that are ungodly among them of all their ungodly deeds which they have ungodly committed, and of all their hard speeches which ungodly sinners have spoken against him.

These are murmurers, complainers, walking after their own lusts; and their mouth speaketh great swelling words, having men's persons in admiration because of advantage.

But, beloved, remember ye the words which were spoken before of the apostles of our Lord Jesus Christ; how that they told you there should be mockers in the last time, who should walk after their own ungodly lusts. These be they who separate themselves, sensual, having not the Spirit.

Jude says a judgment is coming upon these people because the net effect of their work is to cause people to become immoral murmurers and complainers who speak things they do not understand, prefer one person above another, try to gain advantage over other people, and deny the power of faith in Jesus Christ. In Verse 17 he says, "Some of you were alive when the apostles preached and warned you there would be people like this who would mock the things of God, live their own immoral lives, and creep in among you. But you are to be separate from them because they are sensual. Their whole being is controlled by lust — after power, money, and immorality — because they do not have the Spirit of God. Do not be a part of such an unregenerated, unanointed, ungodly group of people."

Jude 20-23

But ye, beloved, building up yourselves on your most holy faith, praying in the Holy Ghost, keep yourselves in the love of God, looking for the mercy of our Lord Jesus Christ unto eternal life. And of some have compassion, making a difference: and others save with fear, pulling them out of the fire; hating even the garment spotted by the flesh.

When Jude gets through issuing the warnings, he says, "Here is what you do. First of all, remember you are beloved of God. Second, build yourselves up in the faith by praying in the Spirit. Third, keep yourselves in the love of God, because you have the power to do it. And fourth, have compassion toward all people, but in a special way toward those in the Body of Christ and those who are willing to hear the Word of God. Reach out to them as if you were pulling them out of the fire, while being careful that your own spiritual life is not spotted by their immorality. In effect, love the sinner but hate the sin. Love the person but hate the wrong he is doing."

Jude 24,25
> Now unto him that is able to keep you from falling, and to present you faultless before the presence of his glory with exceeding joy, to the only wise God our Saviour, be glory and majesty, dominion and power, both now and ever. Amen.

Our God is Able

Jude brings his powerful letter to a close by saying, "Our God is able. Let the forces of this world say their thing, but let them hear: Our God is able. Let the devil come against us with all of his power, but let him know: Our God is able."

I thank God for Jude's advice to you and me. I receive it for my life. And I stand in agreement with you that you will receive it too. I want us to pause, believe God, and pray. Will you join me in prayer?

> *Our Father, Jude tells us we are beloved of You. He says You have delivered to us the faith that You once delivered to the saints. He tells us to earnestly defend it and stand up for it. He tells us to remember the bad things that happened to people who were full of unbelief and rebellion. And he tells us that You are able. Thank You, Father, because You truly are able.*
>
> *And dear friend, I pray for you to grasp the ability, the strength, and the power of God. I pray the Lord will bless you, keep you, heal you, and be with you. Amen and amen.*

The
Revelation of
Saint John the Divine

The
Revelation of
Saint John the Divine

This is a book that speaks to God's people in every generation. And yet, there are people who do not know the book of Revelation is in the Bible. There are ministers of the gospel who never preach one message from it or even refer to it. If we were to ask the typical Christian what the book of Revelation is, he probably would say it is a mystery. But let me tell you, as you and I study it together I predict we will say Revelation is the number-one book in the Bible, because it tells us where we have come from, where we are today, where we are going, and how we are going to get there. I do not denigrate any of the other books of the Bible. But there has to be a consummation — an ending of all things and the beginning of everything anew. Therefore, I pray you will read Revelation and my commentary on it with your mind and your spirit open at all times.

Revelation 1:1-3

The Revelation of Jesus Christ, which God gave unto him, to shew unto his servants things which must shortly come to pass; and he sent and signified it by his angel unto his servant John: who bare record of the word of God, and of the testimony of Jesus Christ, and of all things that he saw.

Blessed is he that readeth, and they that hear the words of this prophecy, and keep those things which are written therein: for the time is at hand.

Introduction

John was in his nineties when he wrote the book of Revelation. He was the last living member of the original twelve apostles. But he, too, would soon become a martyr. For Nero, the ruler of the world from Rome, had become much more active in his persecution of the churches and the Christians. He had killed all the remaining apostles (except John) in one way or another. Thus, John was naturally the most revered and loved Christian in the world at the time. He was looked upon as the leader.

Because Nero hated Christianity so much, he ordered John banished from mankind. The apostle was placed on a little island called Patmos, just off the coast of Turkey. There were no rivers or trees. The only soil able to be cultivated was between the narrow rocky ledges. Patmos was a penal colony where men were banished to be forgotten by the world. Nero no doubt thought that by banishing John, the beloved apostle, he would destroy the whole of Christianity. But God knew where John was. He dispatched His angel to him. And there on that island of loneliness, something stupendous happened.

I want you to notice this book is the Revelation of Jesus Christ which the Father gave to Him. Why did God give it to His Son Jesus? I believe the Father was showing the risen Christ all the things that were to come. So Jesus sent an angel down to John and commanded him to record the revelation for his generation and the generations to come.

John pronounces a blessing on all who read or hear the book of Revelation. (That blessing of God is pronounced upon you, my partner, as you read the book of Revelation and the teaching God has given to me for you.) This is the only book in the Bible that promises a blessing will be upon those who both read and hear it. That puts Revelation in a special category. It is different from all the other books of the Bible.

I personally believe the book of Revelation is written for the most part in code. It is written in code so that it can be deciphered and understood only by those who believe in Jesus Christ as their personal Savior and who, by the Holy Spirit, seek to understand and obey God, so that through them the message of the book can be shared with the world. Thus, if we are to understand Revelation, we have to get in the Spirit.

Revelation 1:4-6

> John to the seven churches which are in Asia: Grace be unto you, and peace, from him which is, and which was, and which is to come; and from the seven Spirits which are before his throne; and from Jesus Christ, who is the faithful witness, and the first begotten of the dead, and the prince of the kings of the earth. Unto him that loved us, and washed us from our sins in his own blood, and hath made us

kings and priests unto God and his Father; to him be glory and dominion for ever and ever. Amen.

The book of Revelation was not written just to these seven specific churches. They were selected from God's standpoint to be reflective and representative of what God was saying to all of His churches throughout the centuries. In addition, everything God said to one of these churches He says in some way to every church, minister, layperson, and believer today.

Revelation 1:7,8

Behold, he cometh with clouds; and every eye shall see him, and they also which pierced him: and all kindreds of the earth shall wail because of him. Even so, Amen.

I am Alpha and Omega, the beginning and the ending, saith the Lord, which is, and which was, and which is to come, the Almighty.

A to Z

Not until John writes the Revelation does Jesus officially proclaim himself the A and the Z, or the Alpha and the Omega — the starting and conclusion of it all.

Revelation 1:9-20

I John, who also am your brother, and companion in tribulation, and in the kingdom and patience of Jesus Christ, was in the isle that is called Patmos, for the word of God, and for the testimony of Jesus Christ.

I was in the Spirit on the Lord's day, and heard behind me a great voice, as of a trumpet, saying, I am Alpha and Omega, the first and the last: and, What thou seest, write in a book, and send it unto the seven churches which are in Asia; unto Ephesus, and unto Smyrna, and unto Pergamos, and unto Thyatira, and unto Sardis, and unto Philadelphia, and unto Laodicea.

And I turned to see the voice that spake with me. And being turned, I saw seven golden candlesticks; and in the midst of the seven candlesticks one like unto the Son of man, clothed with a garment down to the foot, and girt about the paps with a golden girdle.

His head and his hairs were white like wool, as white as snow; and his eyes were as a flame of fire; and his feet like unto fine brass, as if they burned in a furnace; and his voice as the sound of many waters. And he had in his right hand seven stars: and out of his mouth went a sharp twoedged sword: and his countenance was as the sun shineth in his strength.

And when I saw him, I fell at his feet as dead. And he laid his right hand upon me, saying unto me, Fear not; I am the first and the last: I am he that liveth, and was dead; and, behold, I am alive for evermore, Amen; and have the keys of hell and of death.

Write the things which thou hast seen, and the things which are, and the things which shall be hereafter; the mystery of the seven stars which thou sawest in my right hand, and the seven golden candlesticks. The seven stars are the angels of the seven churches: and the seven candlesticks which thou sawest are the seven churches.

The Vision on Patmos

I believe we need to pay special attention to what John is saying about being in the Spirit. In the Spirit means John was wholly free from the earth's influences and was carried by the Spirit into the future. The Spirit allowed him to see the future of the believers and the Church of Jesus Christ. But he could only see the vision while he was in the Spirit. It was a position of utmost clarity that enabled him to receive from the hand of the angel the entire book of Revelation. It was on the Lord's day, the first day of the week, that he was in the Spirit and received this vision.

I want to point out that John saw many symbols in the course of the vision. He saw four winds, seven stars, seven lamps of fire, seven horns, seven eyes, seven heads, and seven mountains. He saw colors like white, red, purple, and black. He saw many animate things such as the lamb, the beast, the dragon, the white horse rider, the red horse rider, the black horse rider, the pale horse rider, and the man-child. He also saw inanimate things such as a rod of iron, many waters, the sword, and the river of life. In addition, he used the number seven a total of 54 times. He speaks of seven spirits of God, seven churches, seven angels, seven seals, seven thunders, seven dooms, seven new things, and many other sevens.

We are told John was instructed to write what he saw and then send it to the seven churches. It is rather miraculous that on a prison island, where he had to work in the mines with the other prisoners, John could find the time and the materials with which to write. How did he do it? We do not know. All we know is that John was somehow able to record the Revelation of Jesus Christ that was given to him. And you and I benefit from his efforts as we study the book of Revelation together.

In Verse 11, John identifies the seven representative churches to which he is writing. They are the churches at Ephesus, Smyrna, Pergamos, Thyatira, Sardis, Philadelphia, and Laodicea. He says he heard a strong, powerful voice behind him — a voice like the sound of a trumpet piercing his innermost being — and when he turned to see who it was, he saw seven golden lampstands and an individual like the Son of man standing in the midst of them.

The Son of man refers to the humanity of Jesus Christ, who is God indwelt. In other words, it is the incarnate Son of God standing in the midst of the seven golden lampstands.

The lampstands represent the seven churches in Asia. They show us that we have no light in us except through Jesus Christ. And our churches have no light in them unless Jesus is in their midst. The lampstands are made of gold, the costliest ingredient, just as the believers are the pure gold of the world. Seven refers to the complete church body of every generation and place since the day of Pentecost.

Jesus is seen clothed in an ankle-length garment. There is a golden girdle around His chest, not around His waist. So Jesus is dressed like a king — like the King of kings and Lord of lords. In Verse 14 we are told His head is as white as snow and His eyes like a flame of fire. That means He is filled with infinite knowledge, and His face is burning with a penetrating intensity that is able to bring all hidden things to light and search all hearts with a single glance. It is a look that His enemies fear and will be unable to withstand when He comes the second time. And yet it is a look that is filled with great inspiration and warmth for those who look for His return.

Verse 15 says His feet shine like burning brass and His voice sounds like a torrent of rushing water. Christ's voice carries with it the triumph of the cross, the glory of the resurrection, and the majesty of His eternal reign. Verse 16 speaks of the seven stars in His right hand. These are the angels of the seven churches. It speaks of the two-edged sword coming from Christ's mouth. This is one of the many symbols of Christ's power in battle and judgment. And it says the face of Jesus is so luminous that it gives light as it were to the whole world.

As we end the first chapter of Revelation, I want you to notice the last verse. In this verse the seven golden candlesticks and the seven stars are explained. The foundation is laid for the rest of the book. In Chapters 2 and 3, we see John writing to the angels, or messengers (represented by the seven stars), of the churches in Asia (represented by the seven golden lampstands). John is told the very words of Jesus to write to the churches. So, what is written comes directly from Jesus Christ and consists of praise, commendation, correction, and sometimes judgment. These are the last recorded words of Jesus to His churches. They are personally addressed to groups of believers in specific congregations.

I want to remind you that these seven churches are literal churches — they existed at the time of John. And yet, they are representative of all churches in all nations from John's time until the second coming of Christ. Also, the seven messages are representative of Jesus' words to all of His churches and believers, from John until now and from our day until Jesus returns.

Revelation 2:1-7

> Unto the angel of the church of Ephesus write; These things saith he that holdeth the seven stars in his right hand, who walketh in the midst of the seven golden candlesticks; I know thy works, and thy labour, and thy patience, and how thou canst not bear them which are evil: and thou hast tried them which say they are apostles, and are not, and hast found them liars: and hast borne, and hast patience, and for my name's sake hast laboured, and hast not fainted.
>
> Nevertheless I have somewhat against thee, because thou hast left thy first love. Remember therefore from whence thou art fallen, and repent, and do the first works; or else I will come unto thee quickly, and will remove thy candlestick out of his place, except thou repent. But this thou hast, that thou hatest the deeds of the Nicolaitanes, which I also hate.
>
> He that hath an ear, let him hear what the Spirit saith unto the churches; To him that overcometh will I give to eat of the tree of life, which is in the midst of the paradise of God.

The Remedy for Love Deficiency

The church at Ephesus began as an anointed, spiritual church. It was one of the most obedient of all the Christian churches. It was a mighty church. But when Jesus looked at the Ephesian congregation some 40 years later, He found a different situation. Yes, He saw their works of labor, their opposition to sin, their faithfulness, and their discipline. He saw how they endured persecution, bore one another's burdens, and hated the things He hated. But He found a fatal deficiency: They had lost their first love. How could Jesus point out all the good things about them and then say that unless they repented, they would lose out? He could do that because Jesus is love. The Ephesian Christians were not allowing Him to fill their lives with His essential nature — love. They were becoming a loveless group of people who said Jesus had changed their lives but who refused to keep on loving and putting Him first. Their only remedy was repentance.

Partner, repentance is squarely facing how we have lost out with God. It is taking responsibility for our actions. When we do that, the Bible promises a godly sorrow that will lead us to truly repent until we actually return to God and recapture the love of Christ. Jesus is saying we can do something to change the loveless condition we may be in.

The message the Lord writes to His churches today is "Love Jesus first." Put Jesus above all forms of worship and all outward displays of religious endeavor. Because Jesus is love. And Jesus is Lord.

Revelation 2:8-11

And unto the angel of the church in Smyrna write; These things saith the first and the last, which was dead, and is alive; I know thy works, and tribulation, and poverty, (but thou art rich) and I know the blasphemy of them which say they are Jews, and are not, but are the synagogue of Satan.

Fear none of those things which thou shalt suffer: behold, the devil shall cast some of you into prison, that ye may be tried; and ye shall have tribulation ten days; be thou faithful unto death, and I will give thee a crown of life.

He that hath an ear, let him hear what the Spirit saith unto the churches; He that overcometh shall not be hurt of the second death.

Faithful Unto Death

There was a large Jewish colony in Smyrna that openly blasphemed the name of Jesus. They did not accept the statement that Jesus Christ is the first and the last, He was dead and is alive. And yet, the Christian congregation in Smyrna was allowing these Jews to join the church, even if they rejected the reality of Jesus Christ. The church really wanted members, especially prestigious Jewish members.

In addition, the long arm of Nero, the Caesar in Rome, had reached Smyrna. Nero's claims to be a god ran counter to the claims of Smyrna believers. They resisted his command to call Caesar lord, saying, "Jesus is Lord." Even when Nero had their property confiscated, they refused to leave Jesus and call Caesar lord.

Jesus praised them for their good stand. He said, "Fear none of the things you will suffer. The devil will cause some of you to be imprisoned and tried. But be faithful unto death and you will receive a crown of life."

Sixty years after John wrote Revelation and it was delivered to the church at Smyrna, the bishop known as Policarp was martyred.

111

The Romans came in and gave him the choice of cursing Jesus and bowing to the name of Caesar or dying. But Policarp looked at them and said, "Eighty and six years have I served the Lord Jesus and He has done me no wrong. How can I blaspheme the King who saved me?" As they bound him to the stake, he said, "You do not have to bind me. I will be here. And the Lord Jesus who has been with me all these years will stand by me." They loosely bound him and he died with a prayer on his lips. For he took literally what Christ had said: "Be thou faithful unto death, and I will give thee a crown of life."

Revelation 2:12-17

And to the angel of the church in Pergamos write; These things saith he which hath the sharp sword with two edges; I know thy works, and where thou dwellest, even where Satan's seat is: and thou holdest fast my name, and hast not denied my faith, even in those days wherein Antipas was my faithful martyr, who was slain among you, where Satan dwelleth.

But I have a few things against thee, because thou hast there them that hold the doctrine of Balaam, who taught Balac to cast a stumblingblock before the children of Israel, to eat things sacrificed unto idols, and to commit fornication.

So hast thou also them that hold the doctrine of the Nicolaitanes, which thing I hate. Repent; or else I will come unto thee quickly, and will fight against them with the sword of my mouth.

He that hath an ear, let him hear what the Spirit saith unto the churches; To him that overcometh will I give to eat of the hidden manna, and will give him a white stone, and in the stone a new name written, which no man knoweth saving he that receiveth it.

The Seat of Satan

Pergamos was a city that followed the Greek god of healing, Asclepias. The temples of Asclepias were all over the city. People flocked to them for the relief of sickness. But the Christians of Pergamos resisted this pagan form of healing because it was linked to idolatry. In fact, Jesus called Pergamos the seat of Satan.

In Verse 12, Jesus was referred to as "He who has the sharp sword with two edges." The Roman proconsul in Pergamos had what was called "the right of the sword." On his word alone, a man could be executed on the spot. But John was told to instruct the believers in Pergamos to not forget that the last word was still with the risen Christ who had the sharp sword with the two edges. For Jesus' sword was greater than all the swords of Satan and man. The believers could trust their lives to Him.

The doctrine of Balaam was referred to in Verse 14.

When the children of Israel were on their wilderness journey from Egypt to the Promised Land, they had to pass through the nation of Moab. Barak, the king of Moab, went to Balaam the prophet and got him to lead Israel into a compromising position. The young men of Israel went in to the young women of Moab, worshiped their idol gods, and committed fornication with them. So, great judgment fell on the people.

The doctrine of the Balaamites was found in the church at Smyrna. The Balaamites tried to teach the Christians that there was nothing incompatible about being a Christian and at the same time conforming to the world's life-style and standards. But Jesus told the believers to avoid the doctrine of the Balaamites. The spirit of the Balaamites was a spirit of compromise, and Jesus stood against spiritual compromise.

Revelation 2:18-29

And unto the angel of the church in Thyatira write; These things saith the Son of God, who hath his eyes like unto a flame of fire, and his feet are like fine brass; I know thy works, and charity, and service, and faith, and thy patience, and thy works; and the last to be more than the first.

Notwithstanding I have a few things against thee, because thou sufferest that woman Jezebel, which calleth herself a prophetess, to teach and to seduce my servants to commit fornication, and to eat things sacrificed unto idols. And I gave her space to repent of her fornication; and she repented not.

Behold, I will cast her into a bed, and them that commit adultery with her into great tribulation, except they repent of their deeds. And I will kill her children with death; and all the churches shall know that I am he which searcheth the reins and hearts: and I will give unto every one of you according to your works.

But unto you I say, and unto the rest in Thyatira, as many as have not this doctrine, and which have not known the depths of Satan, as they speak; I will put upon you none other burden. But that which ye have already hold fast till I come.

And he that overcometh, and keepeth my works unto the end, to him will I give power over the nations: and he shall rule them with a rod of iron; as the vessels of a potter shall they be broken to shivers: even as I received of my Father. And I will give him the morning star.

He that hath an ear, let him hear what the Spirit saith unto the churches.

Jezebel, Purple, and the Church

Thyatira was a prosperous city. And unlike the other six cities mentioned in Chapters 2 and 3, it was fairly free from both Roman and Greek influences. There was no threat of persecution hanging over the church. The believers knew very little about what it meant to suffer for the Lord Jesus Christ.

In those days, it was virtually impossible to create the color purple. But the people of Thyatira had achieved it. They made a very rare and expensive dye with which they colored the clothes worn by Caesar and the nobles of the world. They also used it in the clothes that were draped over their idol gods.

A severe problem resulted from the selling of purple clothes in the church at Thyatira. A very influential and rich woman by the name of Jezebel had joined the church. She represented the wealth and prosperity of the purple dye. She was clothed with garments of purple and helped to drape the idol gods. Her influence became so great in the church that many of the believers followed her into fornication and idol worship. So when Jesus spoke to the church through John, He said, "I have given Jezebel the opportunity to repent, and she refused it. Therefore, I am about to bring judgment upon her and those who follow her."

To the rest of the church, Jesus said, "Hold fast till I come. For I will give you power over the nations and the morning star if you overcome and keep doing My works to the end."

Revelation 3:1-6

And unto the angel of the church in Sardis write; These things saith he that hath the seven Spirits of God, and the seven stars; I know thy works, that thou hast a name that thou livest, and art dead. Be watchful, and strengthen the things which remain that are ready to die: for I have not found thy works perfect before God.

Remember therefore how thou hast received and heard, and hold fast, and repent. If therefore thou shalt not watch, I will come on thee as a thief, and thou shalt not know what hour I will come upon thee. Thou hast a few names even in Sardis which have not defiled their garments; and they shall walk with me in white: for they are worthy.

He that overcometh, the same shall be clothed in white raiment; and I will not blot out his name out of the book of life, but I will confess his name before my Father, and before his angels.

He that hath an ear, let him hear what the Spirit saith unto the churches.

The Results of Opposition

It is peculiar that no mention is made of opposition or persecution against the church at Sardis. I believe that when there is no opposition against the people of God, they probably will not develop. For when the devil comes against us, we stand up in the Spirit of the living God. There is conflict. Our spiritual muscles become hard. Our determination becomes strong. And we discover whether or not we have the Spirit of God.

Jesus tells the believers at Sardis to repent. This is a recurring theme in Christ's message to the seven churches in Asia. He says, "Repent, because I may come to you as a thief in the night. You will not know the hour. For the thief comes when no one expects him. So get yourselves straight with God."

Yet, in Verse 4, Jesus is quick to point out that a small remnant in the church is still true to Him. They are the ones who keep the church going. So He holds before them their reward. The Lord says, "He who overcomes will be clothed in pure white garments. I will not blot your name out of the book of life. Rather, I will confess your name before My Father and before His angels." Then He adds again, "Hear what the Spirit is saying to the churches."

Revelation 3:7-13

And to the angel of the church in Philadelphia write; These things saith he that is holy, he that is true, he that hath the key of David, he that openeth, and no man shutteth; and shutteth, and no man openeth; I know thy works: behold, I have set before thee an open door, and no man can shut it: for thou hast a little strength, and hast kept my word, and hast not denied my name.

Behold, I will make them of the synagogue of Satan, which say they are Jews, and are not, but do lie; behold, I will make them to come and worship before thy feet, and to know that I have loved thee. Because thou hast kept the word of my patience, I also will keep thee from the hour of temptation, which shall come upon all the world, to try them that dwell upon the earth.

Behold, I come quickly: hold that fast which thou hast, that no man take thy crown. Him that overcometh will I make a pillar in the temple of my God, and he shall go no more out: and I will write upon him the name of my God, and the name of the city of my God, which is new Jerusalem, which cometh down out of heaven from my God: and I will write upon him my new name.

He that hath an ear, let him hear what the Spirit saith unto the churches.

The Faithful Church

Jesus is speaking to the church at Philadelphia, a small and struggling but loyal church. He says, "I have the key that lets people in and out. I will open the door to you because I know you well. You may not be strong but you are trying to obey. You have not denied My name as some have. No, you have upheld My name. You have stood against the forces of Satan who claim to be My people. Therefore, because you have patiently obeyed and held to My name, I will protect you from the time of great tribulation and temptation that will come upon all the world."

The Lord adds, "I am coming soon. Stay true to God so that no one will take away your crown. If you overcome and stand fast for Me, I will make you a pillar in the temple of My God. You will be secure. I will take the name of God and My own new name and inscribe them in your being."

The Lord is speaking to a congregation typical of the small struggling churches that seemed to be hidden in some corner of town. They are not looked upon as particularly brilliant churches, but they have many obedient people who are faithful to God. The people go with a spiritual attitude and participate in the church service. They go out in the community and do good works. They lift up the name of Jesus. It is indeed sad that Philadelphia is the only one of the seven churches that Jesus could speak of in this manner.

Revelation 3:14-22

And unto the angel of the church of the Laodiceans write; These things saith the Amen, the faithful and true witness, the beginning of the creation of God; I know thy works, that thou art neither cold nor hot: I would thou wert cold or hot. So then because thou art lukewarm, and neither cold nor hot, I will spue thee out of my mouth.

Because thou sayest, I am rich, and increased with goods, and have need of nothing; and knowest not that thou art wretched, and miserable, and poor, and blind, and naked: I counsel thee to buy of me gold tried in the fire, that thou mayest be rich; and white raiment, that thou mayest be clothed, and that the shame of thy nakedness do not appear; and anoint thine eyes with eyesalve, that thou mayest see.

As many as I love, I rebuke and chasten: be zealous therefore, and repent. Behold, I stand at the door, and knock: if any man hear my voice, and open the door, I will come in to him, and will sup with him, and he with me.

To him that overcometh will I grant to sit with me in my throne, even as I also overcame, and am set down with my Father in his throne.

He that hath an ear, let him hear what the Spirit saith unto the churches.

The Lukewarm Church

Laodicea was a great banking center that dealt in gold. It was a great clothing center that exported fashionable clothes. And it was a great medical center that boasted a medical school and a famous eye clinic where blindness was treated.

Jesus uses these three things in His advice to the Laodicean Christians. He says in Verse 18, "I counsel you to buy gold from Me. Not the gold that the town of Laodicea is dealing with, but real gold — your faith that you release to God for miracles and deliverance. That faith is more precious than all the gold of Laodicea. Also, since you like to brag about your clothing, let Me tell you about the white garments you should be wearing — the fine linen of righteousness. Finally, you talk about your medical school and your excellent eye clinic, but let Me tell you about a different kind of eye medicine — the kind that will restore your spiritual vision so you can see what you can be and do for God."

Jesus gives a special plea in Verses 19 and 20. He says, "As many as I love, I reprove and chasten." Jesus loves these people. They are just lukewarm. They are merely drifting along, week after week, accomplishing nothing. But He says, "I love you. That is why I am giving you this reproof and chastening. And because I love you, I want to tell you that unless you turn from your indifference and become enthusiastic about the things of God, I will chasten you as you have never been chastened." He goes even further and says, "Look, I am standing at your door and I am knocking. I cannot come in until you open the door from the inside. Please let Me in."

Summary of the Seven Churches

I would like to briefly summarize the seven churches for you. The Ephesian Christians had left their first love. They no longer had that throbbing love for Jesus. So He counseled them to repent. And He offered to those who would obey Him the privilege of eating from the tree of life.

The church at Smyrna looked for prestigious members. They wanted to grow and be prestigious in the community. They did not require a personal conversion and faith in the Lord Jesus Christ.

Jesus said to those who would repent, "If you overcome, I will give you a crown of life."

The church at Pergamos was directly affected by the Roman government. There was severe persecution. Jesus commended them for standing up to the persecution, but He said, "I do have something against you because you have allowed the Balaamites to come in and lead you into immorality and idol worship. You have compromised and gone after the things of this world. But if you repent, I will give you a new name and the hidden manna that will sustain you in the midst of the good and the bad."

The church at Thyatira had kept all the outward religious forms but had listened to teachers who denied that Jesus Christ is the Son of God. They were a shell of a church. But Jesus said, "There is a remnant among you and they believe in My name. They are alive in Christ. To you who overcome I will give the privilege of ruling with Me over the nations."

The next church was the church at Sardis. They once had been alive in Christ. But they were now a dead church; there was no life of God in their midst. Yet Jesus saw the remnant. He offered the church another chance to repent and said, "Those who overcome I will clothe in white raiment. I will not blot out your name, but I will personally stand up and speak your name to My Father and His angels."

Jesus did not have any problems with the church at Philadelphia. They were not an overpoweringly strong church, but in their hearts they loved Jesus, they were serving Him, and they were lifting up His name. The Lord said, "I will keep you in the hour of temptation and will make those who overcome a pillar in the temple of God."

Laodicea was the last of the seven churches. It was a lukewarm group of people who did not care about Jesus' claims upon their lives. The Lord was disturbed because of them. He said, "You are neither hot nor cold. It is time that you did something because if you do not, I will spew you out of My mouth. But I want to tell you that I am standing at your door. If you open to Me, I will come in and fellowship with you. And those who overcome I will set with Me on My throne, and they will reign with Me."

Revelation 4:1-11

> After this I looked, and, behold, a door was opened in heaven: and the first voice which I heard was as it were of a trumpet talking with me; which said, Come up hither, and I will shew thee things which must be hereafter.
>
> And immediately I was in the spirit: and, behold, a throne was set in heaven, and one sat on the throne. And he that sat was to look

upon like a jasper and a sardine stone: and there was a rainbow round about the throne, in sight like unto an emerald.

And round about the throne were four and twenty seats: and upon the seats I saw four and twenty elders sitting, clothed in white raiment; and they had on their heads crowns of gold. And out of the throne proceeded lightnings and thunderings and voices: and there were seven lamps of fire burning before the throne, which are the seven Spirits of God.

And before the throne there was a sea of glass like unto crystal: and in the midst of the throne, and round about the throne, were four beasts full of eyes before and behind. And the first beast was like a lion, and the second beast like a calf, and the third beast had a face as a man, and the fourth beast was like a flying eagle.

And the four beasts had each of them six wings about him; and they were full of eyes within: and they rest not day and night, saying, Holy, holy, holy, Lord God Almighty, which was, and is, and is to come.

And when those beasts give glory and honour and thanks to him that sat on the throne, who liveth for ever and ever, the four and twenty elders fall down before him that sat on the throne, and worship him that liveth for ever and ever, and cast their crowns before the throne, saying, Thou art worthy, O Lord, to receive glory and honour and power: for thou hast created all things, and for thy pleasure they are and were created.

John's Vision of God's Throne

John is given a vision of heaven in all of its splendor. There is God on His throne, situated in a sea of glass, which represents light. Round about are His created beings. As these marvelous creatures surround the throne of God, they see Him in all of His glory and recognize He is God. They burst out with shouts of "Holy, holy, holy, Lord God Almighty." The 24 elders are so swept up in the glory of God and the praise coming from their hearts that they take the gold crowns from their heads and cast them at His feet. The chorus swells with "Thou art worthy, O Lord, to receive honor, glory, and power, for You have created all things."

Friend, we are created to glorify God and enjoy Him forever. Whatever we do is to be an act of praise to the spotless Lamb of God, Jesus Christ, to the Father who sits on His throne in heaven, and to the Holy Spirit who indwells us forevermore. Everything we do on earth comes second to giving praise to God. The Bible says that God inhabits the praises of His people. And as we praise Him, we endure with Him, and nothing can take away our relationship with Him.

Revelation 5:1-14

And I saw in the right hand of him that sat on the throne a book written within and on the backside, sealed with seven seals. And I saw a strong angel proclaiming with a loud voice, Who is worthy to open the book, and to loose the seals thereof? And no man in heaven, nor in earth, neither under the earth, was able to open the book, neither to look thereon.

And I wept much, because no man was found worthy to open and to read the book, neither to look thereon. And one of the elders saith unto me, Weep not: behold, the Lion of the tribe of Juda, the Root of David, hath prevailed to open the book, and to loose the seven seals thereof.

And I beheld, and, lo, in the midst of the throne and of the four beasts, and in the midst of the elders, stood a Lamb as it had been slain, having seven horns and seven eyes, which are the seven Spirits of God sent forth into all the earth. And he came and took the book out of the right hand of him that sat upon the throne. And when he had taken the book, the four beasts and four and twenty elders fell down before the Lamb, having every one of them harps, and golden vials full of odours, which are the prayers of saints.

And they sung a new song, saying, Thou art worthy to take the book, and to open the seals thereof: for thou wast slain, and hast redeemed us to God by thy blood out of every kindred, and tongue, and people, and nation; and hast made us unto our God kings and priests; and we shall reign on the earth.

And I beheld, and I heard the voice of many angels round about the throne and the beasts and the elders: and the number of them was ten thousand times ten thousand, and thousands of thousands; saying with a loud voice, Worthy is the Lamb that was slain to receive power, and riches, and wisdom, and strength, and honour, and glory, and blessing.

And every creature which is in heaven, and on the earth, and under the earth, and such as are in the sea, and all that are in them, heard I saying, Blessing, and honour, and glory, and power, be unto him that sitteth upon the throne, and unto the Lamb for ever and ever. And the four beasts said, Amen. And the four and twenty elders fell down and worshipped him that liveth for ever and ever.

The Book with Seven Seals

The fifth chapter opens with John seeing God on the throne, holding a book in His hand. It is sealed with seven seals. And the question is, What is in that book? What is so tremendous about someone being able to open it and reveal its contents?

First of all, God has a design for His universe and His people, and it is all contained in this book. His will and last testament are there to be spelled out for mankind. Second, God is going to measure the world, the nations, and all people by what is in this book.

The book captures the attention of all the creatures around the throne of God. And when John sees that no one can open it and reveal its contents, he begins to weep. But he hears a voice saying, "Do not cry, John. There is someone coming called the Lion of the tribe of Judah. He is able to open the book."

This is one of the most significant and historic scenes in the Word of God. John is caught up by the Spirit and is able to look into the infinite future. He can see God on His throne in a sea of light, surrounded by glorious creatures representative of all the things God has created. He is told not to cry because God's Son has prevailed and the victory has been won. For on Calvary the Lamb was put to death, but He is raised from the dead and is coming to unseal the will and purpose of God.

The Lamb has seven horns and seven eyes. The horns stand for the power and omnipotence of God. The eyes stand for the insight and perfect understanding of God. So the Lamb is there, still carrying the wounds of Calvary, but clothed in the power and omnipotence of God. And He is worthy to be praised — by heavenly creatures, by the 24 elders, by angels, and by every living thing in heaven and on earth.

Revelation 6:1,2
> And I saw when the Lamb opened one of the seals, and I heard, as it were the noise of thunder, one of the four beasts saying, Come and see. And I saw, and behold a white horse: and he that sat on him had a bow; and a crown was given unto him: and he went forth conquering, and to conquer.

As the seals are opened, we will see four different horses, beginning with a white horse. The main thing to see in the opening of the first seal is that there is the spread of war throughout the earth.

Revelation 6:3,4
> And when he had opened the second seal, I heard the second beast

say, Come and see. And there went out another horse that was red:
and power was given to him that sat thereon to take peace from the
earth, and that they should kill one another: and there was given unto
him a great sword.

The appearance of the red horse rider taking peace from the earth
is a direct reference to what happens when peace is taken from a
race, a social class, or any group of people. When their peace is
gone, they turn upon one another or others and begin to kill them.

Revelation 6:5,6
And when he had opened the third seal, I heard the third beast say,
Come and see. And I beheld, and lo a black horse; and he that sat on
him had a pair of balances in his hand. And I heard a voice in the
midst of the four beasts say, A measure of wheat for a penny, and
three measures of barley for a penny; and see thou hurt not the oil
and the wine.

Famine, hunger, and inflation have ravaged the people of our
world. In some parts of the world people spend a full day's wages
just to eat. Many of them could not buy enough to eat and have
starved to death by the tens of millions. But in the great tribulation
period, when Antichrist comes, this will be greatly accelerated.

A voice says in Verse 6, "And see thou hurt not the oil and the
wine." The economy and food supply of the Middle East consisted
of three things at that time: grain, oil, and wine. Grain was the basic
food source while oil and wine were the luxuries. So the voice from
the midst of the beasts is saying that men will have great luxuries,
but will not be able to fill their stomachs. In the tribulation there
will be a time when food will disappear from the earth. The pounding
of the earth by the forces of war will prevent the earth from bringing
forth its food supply. And people will die by the hundreds of millions.

Revelation 6:7,8
And when he had opened the fourth seal, I heard the voice of the
fourth beast say, Come and see. And I looked, and behold a pale
horse: and his name that sat on him was Death, and Hell followed
with him. And power was given unto them over the fourth part of the
earth, to kill with sword, and with hunger, and with death, and with
the beasts of the earth.

The rider of the pale horse will have the power to destroy a fourth
of the human population through war, death, hunger, and the beasts
leaving their forests to kill human beings because there no longer

is food for them in their natural habitat. This is pointing to what will happen when sin reaches its fullness, when the man of sin, Antichrist, is revealed, and when the devil has sway over the world.

Revelation 6:9-11

> And when he had opened the fifth seal, I saw under the altar the souls of them that were slain for the word of God, and for the testimony which they held: and they cried with a loud voice, saying, How long, O Lord, holy and true, dost thou not judge and avenge our blood on them that dwell on the earth? And white robes were given unto every one of them; and it was said unto them, that they should rest yet for a little season, until their fellowservants also and their brethren, that should be killed as they were, should be fulfilled.

Notice there is an altar in heaven and under it are the souls of those who were slain because of the Word of God they believed in and the testimony they gave. The martyrs are crying out to God to avenge their blood upon those who dwell on the earth.

Notice also that those who have been martyred for Christ and whose souls are in heaven are more alive than they have ever been. There is a doctrine that says that when a person dies, his spirit or soul does not go to heaven at all; it goes into a sleep and has no activity until the resurrection. But the Bible does not teach soul sleep. The Bible teaches that when we die, our souls are absent from the body and present with the Lord. Here is a great example of that. Those who have been martyred are in heaven, they are talking with the Lord, white robes are given to them, and they are told to wait until all of their number is completed.

Revelation 6:12-17

> And I beheld when he had opened the sixth seal, and, lo, there was a great earthquake; and the sun became black as sackcloth of hair, and the moon became as blood; and the stars of heaven fell unto the earth, even as a fig tree casteth her untimely figs, when she is shaken of a mighty wind. And the heaven departed as a scroll when it is rolled together; and every mountain and island were moved out of their places.
>
> And the kings of the earth, and the great men, and the rich men, and the chief captains, and the mighty men, and every bondman, and every free man, hid themselves in the dens and in the rocks of the mountains; and said to the mountains and rocks, Fall on us, and hide us from the face of him that sitteth on the throne, and from the wrath of the Lamb: for the great day of his wrath is come; and who shall be able to stand?

The Terror of the Sixth Seal

I want to direct your attention to what Jesus said in Matthew 24:29,30:

"Immediately after the tribulation of those days shall the sun be darkened, and the moon shall not give her light, and the stars shall fall from heaven, and the powers of the heavens shall be shaken: and then shall appear the sign of the Son of man in heaven: and then shall all the tribes of the earth mourn, and they shall see the Son of man coming in the clouds of heaven with power and great glory."

Notice that what Jesus said in Matthew 24 corresponds with what John saw when the sixth seal was opened. Somewhere during the tribulation period, the sixth seal will be opened and a tremendous earthquake will tear at the earth. There will be a disturbance of the elements in outer space. The sun, moon, and stars will be greatly diminished so they will not give their normal light. The heavens will begin to depart. The mountains and islands will begin to shift in their places upon the earth. And the leaders of the world who followed Antichrist in rebellion against Jesus Christ will see these events as a danger to themselves. They will cry out in fear to be hidden from the face of our God who sits on the throne and from the wrath of the Lamb of God.

I personally believe that between the opening of the fifth and sixth seals, many mighty events will take place. By this time the midpoint of the great tribulation period will have arrived. Antichrist will have made a covenant with the Jewish people to restore the temple and reestablish their worship. But he will break his covenant with them. He will go into the temple and desecrate it by setting up an image of himself. He will declare he is the messiah of the Jews.

But the eyes of the Jews will be opened and they will reject him. For written in the law is the commandment to not bow down to any graven image. So the wrath of Antichrist will be poured out against them and everyone else living at that time who missed the secret catching up of the Bride of Christ.

Antichrist will be energized by the devil himself. There will be a trinity of evil just as there is a trinity of the Godhead. The trinity of evil will be the devil, Antichrist, and Antichrist's false prophet. They will endeavor to stamp out the last vestige of the knowledge of God. But they will find that impossible. For we as human beings are incurably religious. That's because when God created us, He left something of himself in every one of us. And there is no power on earth or in hell below that can take that inner craving for God from us.

Revelation 7:1-8

And after these things I saw four angels standing on the four corners of the earth, holding the four winds of the earth, that the wind should not blow on the earth, nor on the sea, nor on any tree.

And I saw another angel ascending from the east, having the seal of the living God: and he cried with a loud voice to the four angels, to whom it was given to hurt the earth and the sea, saying, Hurt not the earth, neither the sea, nor the trees, till we have sealed the servants of our God in their foreheads.

And I heard the number of them which were sealed: and there were sealed an hundred and forty and four thousand of all the tribes of the children of Israel. Of the tribe of Juda were sealed twelve thousand. Of the tribe of Reuben were sealed twelve thousand. Of the tribe of Gad were sealed twelve thousand. Of the tribe of Asher were sealed twelve thousand. Of the tribe of Nephtalim were sealed twelve thousand. Of the tribe of Manasses were sealed twelve thousand. Of the tribe of Simeon were sealed twelve thousand. Of the tribe of Levi were sealed twelve thousand. Of the tribe of Issachar were sealed twelve thousand. Of the tribe of Zabulon were sealed twelve thousand. Of the tribe of Joseph were sealed twelve thousand. Of the tribe of Benjamin were sealed twelve thousand.

The Sealing of the Jews

The angel is saying, "Hold everything till we seal the Jews who have received Jesus Christ as their personal Savior." Twelve multiplied by 12 gives 144, which is multiplied by 1,000 to give 144,000. This may or may not mean exactly 144,000. It may simply mean that a large number of Jews will accept Jesus Christ. The important thing to remember is that thousands upon thousands of each tribe of Israel will come to Christ.

Revelation 7:9-17

After this I beheld, and, lo, a great multitude, which no man could number, of all nations, and kindreds, and people, and tongues, stood before the throne, and before the Lamb, clothed with white robes, and palms in their hands; and cried with a loud voice, saying, Salvation to our God which sitteth upon the throne, and unto the Lamb.

And all the angels stood round about the throne, and about the elders and the four beasts, and fell before the throne on their faces, and worshipped God, saying, Amen: Blessing, and glory, and wisdom, and thanksgiving, and honour, and power, and might, be unto our God for ever and ever. Amen.

And one of the elders answered, saying unto me, What are these which are arrayed in white robes? and whence came they? And I said unto him, Sir, thou knowest.

And he said to me, These are they which came out of great tribulation, and have washed their robes, and made them white in the blood of the Lamb. Therefore are they before the throne of God, and serve him day and night in his temple: and he that sitteth on the throne shall dwell among them.

They shall hunger no more, neither thirst any more; neither shall the sun light on them, nor any heat. For the Lamb which is in the midst of the throne shall feed them, and shall lead them unto living fountains of waters: and God shall wipe away all tears from their eyes.

The Great Tribulation

My own understanding of the tribulation period is that it is a period of seven years, the first three-and-a-half of which are spent in the rising of Antichrist. During the first three years, he will bring peace to the world and economic recovery to man. He will settle all political disputes and appear almost as a superman who captures the imagination and adoration of the world.

But in the midst of the seven years, his personality and nature will appear to totally change. He will become the world dictator. And then, all hell will break loose upon the earth. Those who refuse to worship Antichrist will be ruthlessly martyred. The world will be in distress as never before.

Revelation 8:1-5

And when he had opened the seventh seal, there was silence in heaven about the space of half an hour. And I saw the seven angels which stood before God; and to them were given seven trumpets.

And another angel came and stood at the altar, having a golden censer; and there was given unto him much incense, that he should offer it with the prayers of all saints upon the golden altar which was before the throne. And the smoke of the incense which came with the prayers of the saints, ascended up before God out of the angel's hand.

And the angel took the censer, and filled it with fire of the altar, and cast it into the earth: and there were voices, and thunderings, and lightnings, and an earthquake.

This chapter opens by saying there is a period of silence in heaven for half an hour. Everything comes to a standstill. The silence means

126

there is no more hope for mankind. For on the one hand, the end of time as we know it is about to be announced by the trumpets. And on the other, all the prayers of God's people are becoming a crescendo as they are spoken to the Lord.

Revelation 8:6-11

And the seven angels which had the seven trumpets prepared themselves to sound.

The first angel sounded, and there followed hail and fire mingled with blood, and they were cast upon the earth: and the third part of trees was burnt up, and all green grass was burnt up.

And the second angel sounded, and as it were a great mountain burning with fire was cast into the sea: and the third part of the sea became blood; and the third part of the creatures which were in the sea, and had life, died; and the third part of the ships were destroyed.

And the third angel sounded, and there fell a great star from heaven, burning as it were a lamp, and it fell upon the third part of the rivers, and upon the fountains of waters; and the name of the star is called Wormwood: and the third part of the waters became wormwood; and many men died of the waters, because they were made bitter.

I think the important thing to notice is that the Lord said in Genesis 9:11 that He would never again destroy the world by water; He would destroy it by fire. And in each of these instances, fire is falling upon the earth and beginning to destroy mankind that does not know God.

Revelation 8:12

And the fourth angel sounded, and the third part of the sun was smitten, and the third part of the moon, and the third part of the stars; so as the third part of them was darkened, and the day shone not for a third part of it, and the night likewise.

This is a further diminishing of the solar system so that the world finds itself with one-third less light. It is prophesied in the Old Testament by Amos the prophet in Amos 8:9. And it is certainly a part of the prophecy of Joel in Joel 2:2-11, which the apostle Peter used on the day of Pentecost to tell what would happen in the last days.

Revelation 8:13-9:12

And I beheld, and heard an angel flying through the midst of heaven, saying with a loud voice, Woe, woe, woe, to the inhabiters of the earth by reason of the other voices of the trumpet of the three angels, which are yet to sound!

And the fifth angel sounded, and I saw a star fall from heaven unto the earth: and to him was given the key of the bottomless pit. And he opened the bottomless pit; and there arose a smoke out of the pit, as the smoke of a great furnace; and the sun and the air were darkened by reason of the smoke of the pit.

And there came out of the smoke locusts upon the earth: and unto them was given power, as the scorpions of the earth have power. And it was commanded them that they should not hurt the grass of the earth, neither any green thing, neither any tree; but only those men which have not the seal of God in their foreheads.

And to them it was given that they should not kill them, but that they should be tormented five months: and their torment was as the torment of a scorpion, when he striketh a man. And in those days shall men seek death, and shall not find it; and shall desire to die, and death shall flee from them.

And the shapes of the locusts were like unto horses prepared unto battle; and on their heads were as it were crowns like gold, and their faces were as the faces of men. And they had hair as the hair of women, and their teeth were as the teeth of lions. And they had breastplates, as it were breastplates of iron; and the sound of their wings was as the sound of chariots of many horses running to battle. And they had tails like unto scorpions, and there were stings in their tails: and their power was to hurt men five months.

And they had a king over them, which is the angel of the bottomless pit, whose name in the Hebrew tongue is Abaddon, but in the Greek tongue hath his name Apollyon. One woe is past; and, behold, there come two woes more hereafter.

The Fifth Trumpet

The ninth chapter of Revelation opens with the fifth angel sounding and a star, or an angel, being forced out of heaven to the earth. He is given the key to the bottomless pit. When he opens the pit the darkness of hell itself comes up, blots out the sun for a season, and pollutes the air. Demonic spirits called locusts are released into the world with a command (meaning they are intelligent beings and can carry out commands) to not hurt the greenery of the earth but only those people who do not have the seal of God in their foreheads.

The ones who are going to be tormented by the demonic spirits are those who have taken the mark of the beast and therefore do not have the seal of God in their foreheads. They will not have repented and become converted during the tribulation period. The demonic spirits will strike these people with chills, fevers, frothing at the mouth, strokes, and unconsciousness. For five months the world will go through this hellish condition — a preview of an everlasting hell.

But those who have the seal of God, who have been washed in the blood of Jesus, will not have to go through this torment. They will not be touched by the evil spirits. I tell you, my friend, if Jesus Christ is your Savior and you know that you know that Jesus is in your life, God will see you through all these things. For I believe that every true born-again child of God will be secretly caught up before the tribulation ever begins.

Revelation 9:13-21

And the sixth angel sounded, and I heard a voice from the four horns of the golden altar which is before God, saying to the sixth angel which had the trumpet, Loose the four angels which are bound in the great river Euphrates.

And the four angels were loosed, which were prepared for an hour, and a day, and a month, and a year, for to slay the third part of men.

And the number of the army of the horsemen were two hundred thousand thousand: and I heard the number of them. And thus I saw the horses in the vision, and them that sat on them, having breastplates of fire, and of jacinth, and brimstone: and the heads of the horses were as the heads of lions; and out of their mouths issued fire and smoke and brimstone.

By these three was the third part of men killed, by the fire, and by the smoke, and by the brimstone, which issued out of their mouths. For their power is in their mouth, and in their tails: for their tails were like unto serpents, and had heads, and with them they do hurt.

And the rest of the men which were not killed by these plagues yet repented not of the works of their hands, that they should not worship devils, and idols of gold, and silver, and brass, and stone, and of wood: which neither can see, nor hear, nor walk: neither repented they of their murders, nor of their sorceries, nor of their fornication, nor of their thefts.

The Sixth Trumpet

John is talking about a universal situation. There are four angels loosed from the area of the Euphrates River and with them is an army of hundreds of millions of demonic spirits. From the mouths of these angels come fire, smoke, and brimstone which kills a third of mankind all over the world. Certainly people in America will be touched right along with those in South America, Europe, Asia, Africa, and all the continents of the earth. And yet, with all the torment that is brought upon the people, they do not repent of their murders, sorceries, witchcrafts, thefts, and fornications.

I would like to stop and pray because I know we all need God. Will you join me in prayer?

> *Heavenly Father, we read this book with great respect. We understand from the book of Revelation that things that are to come to pass are already beginning to happen. We see evidence of that on every hand. So it is time that we let You have Your way in our lives. Oh Lord, forgive us. Deliver us. And help us to exercise our wills toward You so we can resist the devil and turn ourselves completely to Jesus Christ.*
>
> *Dear friend, I pray God will be so close to you that you will be convicted of your sins and will open your heart to believe on the Lord. I pray you will not be like those who do not repent. May you understand to the depths of your being that your only safety is in God. May the Lord richly bless and deliver you. I pray through Jesus Christ our Lord. Amen and amen.*

Revelation 10:1-11

And I saw another mighty angel come down from heaven, clothed with a cloud: and a rainbow was upon his head, and his face was as it were the sun, and his feet as pillars of fire: and he had in his hand a little book open: and he set his right foot upon the sea, and his left foot on the earth, and cried with a loud voice, as when a lion roareth: and when he had cried, seven thunders uttered their voices.

And when the seven thunders had uttered their voices, I was about to write: and I heard a voice from heaven saying unto me, Seal up those things which the seven thunders uttered, and write them not.

And the angel which I saw stand upon the sea and upon the earth lifted up his hand to heaven, and sware by him that liveth for ever and ever, who created heaven, and the things that therein are, and the earth, and the things that therein are, and the sea, and the things which are therein, that there should be time no longer: but in the days of the voice of the seventh angel, when he shall begin to sound, the mystery of God should be finished, as he hath declared to his servants the prophets.

And the voice which I heard from heaven spake unto me again, and said, Go and take the little book which is open in the hand of the angel which standeth upon the sea and upon the earth. And I went unto the angel, and said unto him, Give me the little book. And he said unto me, Take it, and eat it up; and it shall make thy belly bitter, but it shall be in thy mouth sweet as honey.

And I took the little book out of the angel's hand, and ate it up; and it was in my mouth sweet as honey: and as soon as I had eaten it, my belly was bitter. And he said unto me, Thou must prophesy again before many peoples, and nations, and tongues, and kings.

The Angel, the Book, and John

The tenth chapter opens with John seeing a mighty angel come down from heaven clothed with a cloud. The angel is holding a little book that is open. Doubtless, this is the book that contains the plan and purpose of God, as well as the title (or deed) to the earth.

John then has a graphic vision of the mighty angel standing with one foot on land and the other on sea — which signifies covering the whole universe. As the angel stands there he roars like a lion. Thunders peal across the sky. And the words "time shall be no more" are flung into the universe.

At that precise moment there is a releasing of all the forces of sin and all the forces of righteousness which will come to a climax in a matter of only weeks or months. I believe that from this event till Armageddon, when Jesus Christ returns to earth and sets up His rule, is a very short period of time. And the little book in the angel's hand no doubt contains all the events of those days.

Revelation 11:1-14

And there was given me a reed like unto a rod: and the angel stood, saying, Rise, and measure the temple of God, and the altar, and them that worship therein. But the court which is without the temple leave out, and measure it not; for it is given unto the Gentiles: and the holy city shall they tread under foot forty and two months.

And I will give power unto my two witnesses, and they shall prophesy a thousand two hundred and threescore days, clothed in sackcloth. These are the two olive trees, and the two candlesticks standing before the God of the earth.

And if any man will hurt them, fire proceedeth out of their mouth, and devoureth their enemies: and if any man will hurt them, he must in this manner be killed. These have power to shut heaven, that it rain not in the days of their prophecy: and have power over waters to turn them to blood, and to smite the earth with all plagues, as often as they will.

And when they shall have finished their testimony, the beast that ascendeth out of the bottomless pit shall make war against them, and shall overcome them, and kill them. And their dead bodies shall lie in the street of the great city, which spiritually is called Sodom and Egypt, where also our Lord was crucified.

And they of the people and kindreds and tongues and nations shall see their dead bodies three days and an half, and shall not suffer their dead bodies to be put in graves. And they that dwell upon the earth shall rejoice over them, and make merry, and shall send gifts one to another; because these two prophets tormented them that dwelt on the earth.

And after three days and an half the Spirit of life from God entered into them, and they stood upon their feet; and great fear fell upon them which saw them. And they heard a great voice from heaven saying unto them, Come up hither. And they ascended up to heaven in a cloud; and their enemies beheld them.

And the same hour was there a great earthquake, and the tenth part of the city fell, and in the earthquake were slain of men seven thousand: and the remnant were affrighted, and gave glory to the God of heaven.

The second woe is past; and, behold, the third woe cometh quickly.

The Two Witnesses

Let me begin by saying that God always has His witnesses. These two witnesses are compared in Verse 4 to two olive trees and two candlesticks. The oil of the olive tree represents the Holy Spirit. And the candlesticks represent the light or insight of God. So these witnesses are Spirit-filled and have the light, or the understanding, of God's plan and purpose in the world.

Some people believe that one of the witnesses will be Elijah, the greatest prophet in Israel, because he was translated and never saw death. In Malachi 4:5,6, we read:

Behold, I will send you Elijah the prophet before the coming of the great and dreadful day of the Lord: and he shall turn the heart of the fathers to the children, and the heart of the children to their fathers, lest I come and smite the earth with a curse.

Others believe the second witness will be Enoch, who walked with God and pleased Him so much that He took him. That is, God translated Enoch to heaven so that he did not taste death. And since the Bible says, "It is appointed unto men once to die," that means that Enoch, in addition to Elijah, must die. Therefore, some people say, the two witnesses must be Elijah and Enoch.

But I want you to notice Verse 6. The two witnesses have the power to shut heaven so that it does not rain during the days of their prophecy. Remember from the Old Testament it was Elijah

who prayed for the rain to cease, and it did not rain for 42 months.
Go back to Verse 6. The two witnesses also have power over the
waters to turn them to blood and to smite the earth with plagues
as often as they desire. Moses is the one who did that in Egypt.

So I am convinced the second witness is Moses, rather than Enoch.
I believe the two witnesses are Elijah and Moses. But no matter who
they are, they certainly are Spirit-filled. They have the insight of
God. They work miracles. And when the forces of Antichrist come
against them during their testimony, they destroy them with fire
from their mouths.

What is the significance of the two witnesses being on the earth
during the tribulation? God says in His Word that He is not willing
for any person to perish. He wants everyone to repent and come
into life. So let me go back to my first statement. I believe God
always has His witnesses. Even in the midst of the end, when it looks
as if the world has absolutely refused God and all appears to be
lost, God still holds on. He sends the two that can do the most. And
they are highly successful. They help ignite a tremendous revival
around the world. No doubt many millions of people will have the
spiritual strength to resist the mark of the beast because of the
witness of these two men. And because of them, millions will be
sealed by God into everlasting salvation.

Revelation 11:15-19

> And the seventh angel sounded; and there were great voices in heaven,
> saying, The kingdoms of this world are become the kingdoms of our
> Lord, and of his Christ; and he shall reign for ever and ever.
>
> And the four and twenty elders, which sat before God on their seats,
> fell upon their faces, and worshipped God, saying, We give thee thanks,
> O Lord God Almighty, which art, and wast, and art to come; because
> thou hast taken to thee thy great power, and hast reigned. And the
> nations were angry, and thy wrath is come, and the time of the dead,
> that they should be judged, and that thou shouldest give reward unto
> thy servants the prophets, and to the saints, and them that fear thy
> name, small and great; and shouldest destroy them which destroy
> the earth.
>
> And the temple of God was opened in heaven, and there was seen
> in his temple the ark of his testament: and there were lightnings, and
> voices, and thunderings, and an earthquake, and great hail.

The Seventh Trumpet

When the seventh angel sounds his trumpet, powerful voices in heaven will declare, "The kingdoms of this world have become the kingdoms of God and His Christ, and He shall reign for ever and ever." By now the judgment of the world will have taken place. Armageddon will be over. The Lord will have stepped upon the Mount of Olives and passed through the valley into Jerusalem to be crowned by the saints as King of kings and Lord of lords.

Verse 19 tells us that the temple of God in heaven will be opened and the Ark of the Covenant will be seen as it really is — not the golden box back there in the temple of the Old Testament, but the actual presence of God revealed to His people until they are enveloped by His presence for ever and ever. This great hour will be signified by lightnings, thunderings, and great hail. Physical phenomena will signal the day when the kingdoms of this world become the kingdoms of our Lord.

I would like to add that in the eleventh chapter, John skips over the events of the rest of the book and goes to the last chapter where we win for the glory of God. The events of the eleventh chapter are stated before the details are given in the following chapters. But there is much more to come, friend, that will help us with the details and will have a tremendous influence on the way we live today, tomorrow, and all the days thereafter so we will be ready for the coming of our Lord.

Revelation 12:1-6

> And there appeared a great wonder in heaven; a woman clothed with the sun, and the moon under her feet, and upon her head a crown of twelve stars: and she being with child cried, travailing in birth, and pained to be delivered.
>
> And there appeared another wonder in heaven; and behold a great red dragon, having seven heads and ten horns, and seven crowns upon his heads. And his tail drew the third part of the stars of heaven, and did cast them to the earth: and the dragon stood before the woman which was ready to be delivered, for to devour her child as soon as it was born.
>
> And she brought forth a man child, who was to rule all nations with a rod of iron: and her child was caught up unto God, and to his throne. And the woman fled into the wilderness, where she hath a place prepared of God, that they should feed her there a thousand two hundred and threescore days.

The Woman and the Red Dragon

The most important thing John says to us in the 12th chapter, and continues in the 13th chapter, is that God and His people always triumph. The first six verses set the stage for the victory.

John begins with the beautiful woman clothed in light who represents God's people throughout the ages. She represents Israel. She represents the remnant. She is the faithful one, the one who brought forth Jesus Christ of Nazareth. She is the seed embraced by the Christians. She is the Bride of Christ. She is all of these because the people of God are always referred to as a woman, as the beloved, or as the Bride of Christ.

Then John shows us another side — the ugly red dragon who from the very beginning has attacked the woman. The dragon is the devil. He is Lucifer, the archangel, who rebelled against the Father in heaven. He is the one who rebelled because of his beauty and appointed place, who became proud and said, "I will ascend above the Father and be God." God, however, cannot tolerate sin in heaven, so He cast the devil out. And since the devil is a master of persuasion, he took one-third of the angels with him. Verse four tells us his tail drew the third part of the stars of heaven, the angels, and threw them to the earth.

But the story does not end there. When the devil tries to kill the woman's baby boy, God translates him to His throne where he is safe. And He sends the woman to a place of divine refuge and protection. Then the action really begins.

Revelation 12:7-17

And there was war in heaven: Michael and his angels fought against the dragon; and the dragon fought and his angels, and prevailed not; neither was their place found any more in heaven. And the great dragon was cast out, that old serpent, called the Devil, and Satan, which deceiveth the whole world: he was cast out into the earth, and his angels were cast out with him.

And I heard a loud voice saying in heaven, Now is come salvation, and strength, and the kingdom of our God, and the power of his Christ: for the accuser of our brethren is cast down, which accused them before our God day and night. And they overcame him by the blood of the Lamb, and by the word of their testimony; and they loved not their lives unto the death. Therefore rejoice, ye heavens, and ye that dwell in them. Woe to the inhabitants of the earth and of the sea! for the devil is come down unto you, having great wrath, because he knoweth that he hath but a short time.

And when the dragon saw that he was cast unto the earth, he persecuted the woman which brought forth the man child. And to the woman were given two wings of a great eagle, that she might fly into the wilderness, into her place, where she is nourished for a time, and times, and half a time, from the face of the serpent.

And the serpent cast out of his mouth water as a flood after the woman, that he might cause her to be carried away of the flood. And the earth helped the woman, and the earth opened her mouth, and swallowed up the flood which the dragon cast out of his mouth. And the dragon was wroth with the woman, and went to make war with the remnant of her seed, which keep the commandments of God, and have the testimony of Jesus Christ.

Overcoming the Devil

John graphically describes the war that took place in heaven between Michael and Lucifer. Michael, the one who was assigned to take care of the great remnant of God, fights against Lucifer and prevails over him. The defeated Lucifer is cast to the earth and becomes the devil. Then he begins his persecution of everything that God created. And from the moment people first serve God, the devil is in hot pursuit. He becomes the accuser of the brethren.

During the tribulation period, the devil will know he only has a short time left, so his wrath will be great. In the last years of man's time in this world's system, the devil will come against humanity with all the force that he has ever had. Sin and evil will reach a climax. Brutality will reach its zenith.

But God says in Verse 11 that the devil is able to be overcome. How do we overcome him? We overcome the devil by the shed blood of Christ, which cleanses us from all sin, being applied to our hearts. We overcome him by using the Word of God and the word of our own testimony and by being witnesses for Christ. And we overcome the devil by loving Christ more than we love ourselves, that is, by having the inner attitude that Christ is first in our lives.

Revelation 13:1-10

And I stood upon the sand of the sea, and saw a beast rise up out of the sea, having seven heads and ten horns, and upon his horns ten crowns, and upon his heads the name of blasphemy. And the beast which I saw was like unto a leopard, and his feet were as the feet of a bear, and his mouth as the mouth of a lion: and the dragon gave him his power, and his seat, and great authority.

And I saw one of his heads as it were wounded to death; and his deadly wound was healed: and all the world wondered after the beast. And they worshipped the dragon which gave power unto the beast: and they worshipped the beast, saying, Who is like unto the beast? who is able to make war with him?

And there was given unto him a mouth speaking great things and blasphemies; and power was given unto him to continue forty and two months. And he opened his mouth in blasphemy against God, to blaspheme his name, and his tabernacle, and them that dwell in heaven.

And it was given unto him to make war with the saints, and to overcome them: and power was given him over all kindreds, and tongues, and nations. And all that dwell upon the earth shall worship him, whose names are not written in the book of life of the Lamb slain from the foundation of the world.

If any man have an ear, let him hear. He that leadeth into captivity shall go into captivity: he that killeth with the sword must be killed with the sword. Here is the patience and the faith of the saints.

Antichrist

In the first verse of Chapter 13, John sees Antichrist coming up out of the sand of the sea, which represents the sea of humanity. The beast rises up out of humanity and has seven heads and ten horns. Horns mean power and ten refers to nations. The number seven here means completeness, or total evil. The seven heads all have blasphemy written on them. So Antichrist will be a totally evil person who will begin with ten powerful nations that give him their power or elect him as their head. He will bring such economic and political order that the world will be astounded.

But that is not enough for him to be the real Antichrist. One of his heads will be wounded. Antichrist will be assassinated and the devil will raise him up. Just as God raised His Son from the dead, so the devil will raise his son. Antichrist will then become different. The bestial qualities of the dragon, the devil, will come to the fore in him. But at that precise point another beast enters. And we want to read about him.

Revelation 13:11-18

And I beheld another beast coming up out of the earth; and he had two horns like a lamb, and he spake as a dragon. And he exerciseth all the power of the first beast before him, and causeth the earth and them which dwell therein to worship the first beast, whose deadly wound was healed.

And he doeth great wonders, so that he maketh fire come down from heaven on the earth in the sight of men, and deceiveth them that dwell on the earth by the means of those miracles which he had power to do in the sight of the beast; saying to them that dwell on the earth, that they should make an image to the beast, which had the wound by a sword, and did live.

And he had power to give life unto the image of the beast, that the image of the beast should both speak, and cause that as many as would not worship the image of the beast should be killed. And he causeth all, both small and great, rich and poor, free and bond, to receive a mark in their right hand, or in their foreheads: and that no man might buy or sell, save he that had the mark, or the name of the beast, or the number of his name.

Here is wisdom. Let him that hath understanding count the number of the beast: for it is the number of a man; and his number is Six hundred threescore and six.

The Beast and His Mark

John sees the other beastlike person coming up out of the earth. He has two horns like a lamb but he speaks like a dragon — the devil. He exercises all the power of Antichrist, the first beast. He causes everyone on the earth to worship the first beast whose deadly wound was healed.

Then the Bible says he does great wonders by means of miracles which he performs in the sight of the beast. But I want you to notice one thing: He never performs a miracle the way Christ did. Christ performed miracles to deliver people who were oppressed of the devil. But this man's miracles begin by convincing the world that Antichrist has risen from the dead. In addition, he convinces the world to make an image of the beast. He then gives life to the image so it can speak.

The beast will force everyone to receive a mark either on their right hands or their foreheads. It is the number of a man, 666. Those who do not receive it will not be able to buy or sell. Suppose you go to the grocery store, load your cart, walk to the cash register, and prepare to pay. Then, the cashier looks at your forehead, and the number is not there. He will ask you to hold out your right hand. But the number is not there, either. People will then converge on you from every side and you will either take that mark — and be eternally doomed from the standpoint of God — or refuse to accept it and be taken out and killed. My friend, that will happen someday — maybe sooner than we think.

Revelation 14:1-5

And I looked, and lo, a Lamb stood on the mount Sion, and with him an hundred forty and four thousand, having his Father's name written in their foreheads. And I heard a voice from heaven, as the voice of many waters, and as the voice of a great thunder: and I heard the voice of harpers harping with their harps: and they sung as it were a new song before the throne, and before the four beasts, and the elders: and no man could learn that song but the hundred and forty and four thousand, which were redeemed from the earth.

These are they which were not defiled with women; for they are virgins. These are they which follow the Lamb whithersoever he goeth. These were redeemed from among men, being the firstfruits unto God and to the Lamb. And in their mouth was found no guile: for they are without fault before the throne of God.

When John says, "I looked" or "I saw," it means we begin a new scene. So in Chapter 14 we go from Antichrist, the false prophet, and the red dragon to a new scene that John receives from heaven. I want you to understand that John did not write all of these things in chronological order. Sometimes he looks back or he moves forward into eternity when it was all over. He does not write in a constant vision, but over a period of time.

In Chapter 14, John moves from the midst of the tribulation to give us a scene from above. He shows us the Lamb of God standing on Mount Zion with the firstfruits of the resurrection. The number is noted here as 144,000, but we are not to think that is the limit. For the number is indicative of a massive group of people.

This is a scene of those who will stand with the victorious Savior after the tribulation, Armageddon, the judgment of the nations, and the establishment of Christ's reign. These people are sealed by God during the tribulation because they refused to worship the beast and take his mark.

Revelation 14:6-13

And I saw another angel fly in the midst of heaven, having the everlasting gospel to preach unto them that dwell on the earth, and to every nation, and kindred, and tongue, and people, saying with a loud voice, Fear God, and give glory to him; for the hour of his judgment is come: and worship him that made heaven, and earth, and the sea, and the fountains of waters.

And there followed another angel, saying, Babylon is fallen, is fallen, that great city, because she made all nations drink of the wine of the wrath of her fornication.

And the third angel followed them, saying with a loud voice, If any man worship the beast and his image, and receive his mark in his forehead, or in his hand, the same shall drink of the wine of the wrath of God, which is poured out without mixture into the cup of his indignation; and he shall be tormented with fire and brimstone in the presence of the holy angels, and in the presence of the Lamb: and the smoke of their torment ascendeth up for ever and ever: and they have no rest day nor night, who worship the beast and his image, and whosoever receiveth the mark of his name. Here is the patience of the saints: here are they that keep the commandments of God, and the faith of Jesus.

And I heard a voice from heaven saying unto me, Write, Blessed are the dead which die in the Lord from henceforth: Yea, saith the Spirit, that they may rest from their labours; and their works do follow them.

Three More Angels and Their Messages

John moves from the heavenly scene where the redeemed are worshiping the Lamb to the scene of the tribulation period. He tells of three great angels on a special mission of revival, special news, and judgment. The first angel could be classified as an evangelist. His main message is, "God loves you. He cares for you. And He is reaching out to you." This particular angel comes in the final stages of the tribulation. He appears in the heavens moving from nation to nation, kindred to kindred, and race to race.

The second angel comes and speaks directly to the strongholds of sin. He says, "You are going to be brought down because your evil has reached its climax. The mighty Babylon is destroyed." Babylon represents the strongholds of sin in this world.

The third angel says, "If any man worships the beast and takes his mark, he will drink of the wrath of God and be tormented with fire and brimstone in the presence of the angels and the Lamb of God." The angel is declaring God's judgment for rebellion. He is saying, "The judgment is here and hell is next." The world will soon be in Armageddon where the great battle of the ages will take place.

Revelation 14:14-20

And I looked, and behold a white cloud, and upon the cloud one sat like unto the Son of man, having on his head a golden crown, and in his hand a sharp sickle.

And another angel came out of the temple, crying with a loud voice to him that sat on the cloud, Thrust in thy sickle, and reap: for the time is come for thee to reap; for the harvest of the earth is ripe. And he that sat on the cloud thrust in his sickle on the earth; and the earth was reaped. And another angel came out of the temple which is in heaven, he also having a sharp sickle. And another angel came

out from the altar, which had power over fire; and cried with a loud
cry to him that had the sharp sickle, saying, Thrust in thy sharp sickle,
and gather the clusters of the vine of the earth; for her grapes are
fully ripe.

And the angel thrust in his sickle into the earth, and gathered the
vine of the earth, and cast it into the great winepress of the wrath of
God. And the winepress was trodden without the city, and blood came
out of the winepress, even unto the horse bridles, by the space of a
thousand and six hundred furlongs.

The Battle of Armageddon

When John wrote Revelation, the world did not have the
sophisticated weapons of destruction that we now have or will have
in the future. He is speaking of the battle of Armageddon, that great
war headed by Christ when He comes to fight Antichrist. This is
when the grain will be separated from the chaff, the righteous from
the wicked, and when Christ will crush the last vestiges of the evil
that remains.

Because of this battle, the blood will flow as high as a horse's
bridle. This is a symbolic saying that refers to the length of the
original Palestine, about 200 miles. It simply means that Armageddon
will be the bloodiest hour the world has ever known.

Revelation 15:1

And I saw another sign in heaven, great and marvellous, seven angels
having the seven last plagues; for in them is filled up the wrath of God.

John is shifting the focus again as he shows the last seven plagues
that will come upon sinful man. Notice he says in Verse 2, "And I saw."

Revelation 15:2-4

And I saw as it were a sea of glass mingled with fire: and them that
had gotten the victory over the beast, and over his image, and over
his mark, and over the number of his name, stand on the sea of glass,
having the harps of God.

And they sing the song of Moses the servant of God, and the song
of the Lamb, saying, Great and marvellous are thy works, Lord God
Almighty; just and true are thy ways, thou King of saints. Who shall
not fear thee, O Lord, and glorify thy name? for thou only art holy:
for all nations shall come and worship before thee; for thy judgments
are made manifest.

The Song of Moses

These are the martyrs who come out of the great tribulation. They are singing the song of Moses, found in Exodus 15:1-19. This is the song Moses and the children of Israel sang after they crossed the Red Sea. It simply means the martyrs have crossed over. They are on the other side. They are picking up the language of the saints who have triumphed and are singing it to God.

Revelation 15:5-16:1

And after that I looked, and, behold, the temple of the tabernacle of the testimony in heaven was opened: and the seven angels came out of the temple, having the seven plagues, clothed in pure and white linen, and having their breasts girded with golden girdles.

And one of the four beasts gave unto the seven angels seven golden vials full of the wrath of God, who liveth for ever and ever. And the temple was filled with smoke from the glory of God, and from his power; and no man was able to enter into the temple, till the seven plagues of the seven angels were fulfilled.

And I heard a great voice out of the temple saying to the seven angels, Go your ways, and pour out the vials of the wrath of God upon the earth.

Here we have the angels gathering to pour out the wrath of God. There are two other scenes like this in the Bible. One is when Moses and Aaron brought the plagues down upon Pharaoh and the nation of Egypt. Another is found earlier in this book when the seven trumpets sounded and one-third of the land, sea, fish, water, and ships were destroyed.

Revelation 16:2-7

And the first went, and poured out his vial upon the earth; and there fell a noisome and grievous sore upon the men which had the mark of the beast, and upon them which worshipped his image. And the second angel poured out his vial upon the sea; and it became as the blood of a dead man: and every living soul died in the sea. And the third angel poured out his vial upon the rivers and fountains of waters; and they became blood. And I heard the angel of the waters say, Thou art righteous, O Lord, which art, and wast, and shalt be, because thou hast judged thus. For they have shed the blood of saints and prophets, and thou hast given them blood to drink; for they are worthy. And I heard another out of the altar say, Even so, Lord God Almighty, true and righteous are thy judgments.

The First Three Vials

The first vial is poured upon men and the heat produces vile sores upon their bodies. The second one is poured upon the sea and it becomes as the blood of a dead man. The third vial is poured upon the rivers and fountains of water and they become blood. It is as if the fresh waters have been heated and they, too, become like blood.

In the fifth verse John stops and in effect says, "O Lord, You are judging righteously. These people have shed the blood of Your saints and prophets, so You are giving them blood to drink."

Revelation 16:8-12

And the fourth angel poured out his vial upon the sun; and power was given unto him to scorch men with fire. And men were scorched with great heat, and blasphemed the name of God, which hath power over these plagues: and they repented not to give him glory.

And the fifth angel poured out his vial upon the seat of the beast; and his kingdom was full of darkness; and they gnawed their tongues for pain, and blasphemed the God of heaven because of their pains and their sores, and repented not of their deeds.

And the sixth angel poured out his vial upon the great river Euphrates; and the water thereof was dried up, that the way of the kings of the east might be prepared.

The Fourth, Fifth, and Sixth Vials

The fourth vial is poured upon the sun so that its heat is increased until it literally scorches the earth. Can you imagine what it will be like to set foot upon the earth or touch any part of it? The heat will go right through the flesh.

The fifth angel pours his vial upon the very throne of Antichrist. He touches the light and turns it to darkness. And yet people blaspheme God through all their pains and do not repent. The next vial is poured upon the river Euphrates. The earth becomes a burning planet so hot that it evaporates the river. Can you imagine where man would be if the rivers of the earth evaporated?

Revelation 16:13-16

And I saw three unclean spirits like frogs come out of the mouth of the dragon, and out of the mouth of the beast, and out of the mouth of the false prophet. For they are the spirits of devils, working miracles, which go forth unto the kings of the earth and of the whole world, to gather them to the battle of that great day of God Almighty.

Behold, I come as a thief. Blessed is he that watcheth, and keepeth his garments, lest he walk naked, and they see his shame. And he gathered them together into a place called in the Hebrew tongue Armageddon.

Evil Spirits From the Trinity of Evil

John says, "I saw," so this is another scene. He sees three unclean spirits like frogs coming out of the mouths of the devil, Antichrist, and the false prophet. (The Jews considered frogs unclean. But the people of that day worshiped frogs as symbols of demonic power.) The unclean spirits go throughout the whole earth, gathering the people into the battle of Armageddon. John then inserts a special word from the Lord Jesus Christ.

Armageddon is known throughout the Bible as the place of warfare. Megiddo, the geographical name for Armageddon, is a valley between the Sea of Galilee and the Mediterranean Sea. Whether this means that the entire battle of Armageddon will be confined to this small area, I cannot say. We know from Verse 20 that the armies of all the nations of the world are gathered there. So it is my opinion that this refers to strategic battle areas of the world where Armageddon will be fought.

Revelation 16:17-21

And the seventh angel poured out his vial into the air; and there came a great voice out of the temple of heaven, from the throne, saying, It is done. And there were voices, and thunders, and lightnings; and there was a great earthquake, such as was not since men were upon the earth, so mighty an earthquake, and so great.

And the great city was divided into three parts, and the cities of the nations fell: and great Babylon came in remembrance before God, to give unto her the cup of the wine of the fierceness of his wrath. And every island fled away, and the mountains were not found.

And there fell upon men a great hail out of heaven, every stone about the weight of a talent: and men blasphemed God because of the plague of the hail; for the plague thereof was exceeding great.

The Seventh Vial

The seventh angel actually rains fire out of heaven into the air. There is thunder, lightning, and hail weighing up to 60 pounds that falls on the armies of Antichrist that have come to fight in Armageddon.

Notice in Verse 20 that the fire and brimstone falling upon the earth is so fierce that every island flees away and the mountains are not found. The fire literally changes the form of the earth as we know it today. The earthquakes level the cities of the earth, but the fire burns them up. The earth is entering the process of renovation.

Revelation 17:1-7

> And there came one of the seven angels which had the seven vials, and talked with me, saying unto me, Come hither; I will shew unto thee the judgment of the great whore that sitteth upon many waters: with whom the kings of the earth have committed fornication, and the inhabitants of the earth have been made drunk with the wine of her fornication.
>
> So he carried me away in the spirit into the wilderness: and I saw a woman sit upon a scarlet coloured beast, full of names of blasphemy, having seven heads and ten horns. And the woman was arrayed in purple and scarlet colour, and decked with gold and precious stones and pearls, having a golden cup in her hand full of abominations and filthiness of her fornication: and upon her forehead was a name written, MYSTERY, BABYLON THE GREAT, THE MOTHER OF HARLOTS AND ABOMINATIONS OF THE EARTH.
>
> And I saw the woman drunken with the blood of the saints, and with the blood of the martyrs of Jesus: and when I saw her, I wondered with great admiration. And the angel said unto me, Wherefore didst thou marvel? I will tell thee the mystery of the woman, and of the beast that carrieth her, which hath the seven heads and ten horns.

The thing I want to point out to you in these seven verses is that the woman sits on the beast. She is like a rider on a horse. She is a mysterious figure, but we are going to see that she represents the focal point of power that attaches itself to the beast and makes the beast what he really becomes as Antichrist.

Revelation 17:8-18

> The beast that thou sawest was, and is not; and shall ascend out of the bottomless pit, and go into perdition: and they that dwell on the earth shall wonder, whose names were not written in the book of life from the foundation of the world, when they behold the beast that was, and is not, and yet is. And here is the mind which hath wisdom. The seven heads are seven mountains, on which the woman sitteth.
>
> And there are seven kings: five are fallen, and one is, and the other is not yet come; and when he cometh, he must continue a short space.

And the beast that was, and is not, even he is the eighth, and is of the seven, and goeth into perdition.

And the ten horns which thou sawest are ten kings, which have received no kingdom as yet; but receive power as kings one hour with the beast. These have one mind, and shall give their power and strength unto the beast. These shall make war with the Lamb, and the Lamb shall overcome them: for he is Lord of lords, and King of kings: and they that are with him are called, and chosen, and faithful.

And he saith unto me, The waters which thou sawest, where the whore sitteth, are peoples, and multitudes, and nations, and tongues. And the ten horns which thou sawest upon the beast, these shall hate the whore, and shall make her desolate and naked, and shall eat her flesh, and burn her with fire.

For God hath put in their hearts to fulfil his will, and to agree, and give their kingdom unto the beast, until the words of God shall be fulfilled. And the woman which thou sawest is that great city, which reigneth over the kings of the earth.

The Woman and the Beast

John describes for us the mystery of the woman. In Verse 18 he says the woman is the great city that reigns over the kings of the earth. In other words, the woman is the controlling power and focal point of the end time. But the beast upon which she sits is a group of nations that have come together under one man who carries the number of a man. And from Chapter 13 we know the number of that man is 666.

I believe what John wants us to understand is that the beast, Antichrist, will appear as a brilliant human being. He will bring the nations together and solve their financial and political problems. He will create a false but seemingly genuine peace. Then he will be assassinated. And the false prophet, with the help of the devil, will come on the scene to work his miracles.

Antichrist will not only have natural gifts and talents, he will have supernatural powers. They will be satanic, but they will be supernatural. He will be one that an unsaved, unregenerated world will want. You may ask, "Why would they want such a beast?" It is because they will not want God. They will completely reject God and have a reprobate mind, an apostate mind. So the beast will be attractive to them just as Jesus Christ is to a born-again Christian.

Many people interpret Verse 9 to mean that since Rome is built on seven hills, John must be talking about Rome. I do not. I believe the seven in this verse is the number for completeness — in this particular instance, the completeness of evil. As I have mentioned before, the last days will be the period of time when sin reaches a climax and the tide of evil reaches its fullness. But it will also be the time when righteousness is fulfilled and brings forth the second coming of Christ.

Revelation 18:1-6

And after these things I saw another angel come down from heaven, having great power; and the earth was lightened with his glory. And he cried mightily with a strong voice, saying, Babylon the great is fallen, is fallen, and is become the habitation of devils, and the hold of every foul spirit, and a cage of every unclean and hateful bird. For all nations have drunk of the wine of the wrath of her fornication, and the kings of the earth have committed fornication with her, and the merchants of the earth are waxed rich through the abundance of her delicacies.

And I heard another voice from heaven, saying, Come out of her, my people, that ye be not partakers of her sins, and that ye receive not of her plagues. For her sins have reached unto heaven, and God hath remembered her iniquities.

Reward her even as she rewarded you, and double unto her double according to her works: in the cup which she hath filled fill to her double.

Seed-Faith in Reverse

This is seed-faith in reverse. Babylon the harlot has sown a worldwide evil, so she will reap a worldwide evil. It will be a harvest of damnation, fire, and brimstone. Verse 6 says it will be doubled or increased, just like the principle of seed-faith. The punishment coming upon her is vastly increased over the deeds she has committed.

As you read Verses 7-20, keep in mind that this is the same voice speaking that was introduced in Verse 4.

Revelation 18:7-10

How much she hath glorified herself, and lived deliciously, so much torment and sorrow give her: for she saith in her heart, I sit a queen, and am no widow, and shall see no sorrow.

Therefore shall her plagues come in one day, death, and mourning, and famine; and she shall be utterly burned with fire: for strong is the Lord God who judgeth her.

And the kings of the earth, who have committed fornication and lived deliciously with her, shall bewail her, and lament for her, when they shall see the smoke of her burning, standing afar off for the fear of her torment, saying, Alas, alas that great city Babylon, that mighty city! for in one hour is thy judgment come.

In Chapter 18 of Revelation, just before we get into the final battle called Armageddon, we have the voice from heaven describing the sins of the people of that time. They are living "deliciously." But all of a sudden the world is invaded by the judgment of God and the wages of sin become death.

Revelation 18:11-24

And the merchants of the earth shall weep and mourn over her; for no man buyeth their merchandise any more: the merchandise of gold, and silver, and precious stones, and of pearls, and fine linen, and purple, and silk, and scarlet, and all thyine wood, and all manner vessels of ivory, and all manner vessels of most precious wood, and of brass, and iron, and marble, and cinnamon, and odours, and ointments, and frankincense, and wine, and oil, and fine flour, and wheat, and beasts, and sheep, and horses, and chariots, and slaves, and souls of men.

And the fruits that thy soul lusted after are departed from thee, and all things which were dainty and goodly are departed from thee, and thou shalt find them no more at all. The merchants of these things, which were made rich by her, shall stand afar off for the fear of her torment, weeping and wailing, and saying, Alas, alas that great city, that was clothed in fine linen, and purple, and scarlet, and decked with gold, and precious stones, and pearls!

For in one hour so great riches is come to nought. And every shipmaster, and all the company in ships, and sailors, and as many as trade by sea, stood afar off, and cried when they saw the smoke of her burning, saying, What city is like unto this great city! And they cast dust on their heads, and cried, weeping and wailing, saying, Alas, alas, that great city, wherein were made rich all that had ships in the sea by reason of her costliness! for in one hour is she made desolate.

Rejoice over her, thou heaven, and ye holy apostles and prophets; for God hath avenged you on her.

And a mighty angel took up a stone like a great millstone, and cast it into the sea, saying, Thus with violence shall that great city Babylon be thrown down, and shall be found no more at all. And the voice of harpers, and musicians, and of pipers, and trumpeters, shall be heard no more at all in thee; and no craftsman, of whatsoever craft he be, shall be found any more in thee; and the sound of a millstone shall be heard no more at all in thee; and the light of a candle shall shine no more at all in thee; and the voice of the bridegroom and of the bride shall be heard no more at all in thee: for thy merchants were the great men of the earth; for by thy sorceries were all nations deceived.

And in her was found the blood of prophets, and of saints, and of all that were slain upon the earth.

John vividly portrays the destruction of the world system in Chapter 18. Oh, I tell you, I would rather be a Christian than anything in the world!

My friend, we are ready for Chapter 19 where we will sit down with the Lamb at the marriage supper in heaven and really come into our own.

Revelation 19:1-21

And after these things I heard a great voice of much people in heaven, saying, Alleluia; Salvation, and glory, and honour, and power, unto the Lord our God: for true and righteous are his judgments: for he hath judged the great whore, which did corrupt the earth with her fornication, and hath avenged the blood of his servants at her hand. And again they said, Alleluia. And her smoke rose up for ever and ever.

And the four and twenty elders and the four beasts fell down and worshipped God that sat on the throne, saying, Amen; Alleluia. And a voice came out of the throne, saying, Praise our God, all ye his servants, and ye that fear him, both small and great.

And I heard as it were the voice of a great multitude, and as the voice of many waters, and as the voice of mighty thunderings, saying, Alleluia: for the Lord God omnipotent reigneth. Let us be glad and rejoice, and give honour to him: for the marriage of the Lamb is come, and his wife hath made herself ready. And to her was granted that she should be arrayed in fine linen, clean and white: for the fine linen is the righteousness of saints.

And he saith unto me, Write, Blessed are they which are called unto the marriage supper of the Lamb. And he saith unto me, These are the true sayings of God. And I fell at his feet to worship him. And he said unto me, See thou do it not: I am thy fellowservant, and of thy brethren that have the testimony of Jesus: worship God: for the testimony of Jesus is the spirit of prophecy.

And I saw heaven opened, and behold a white horse; and he that sat upon him was called Faithful and True, and in righteousness he doth judge and make war. His eyes were as a flame of fire, and on his head were many crowns; and he had a name written, that no man knew, but he himself. And he was clothed with a vesture dipped in blood: and his name is called The Word of God.

And the armies which were in heaven followed him upon white horses, clothed in fine linen, white and clean. And out of his mouth goeth a sharp sword, that with it he should smite the nations: and he shall rule them with a rod of iron: and he treadeth the winepress of the fierceness and wrath of Almighty God. And he hath on his vesture and on his thigh a name written, KING OF KINGS, AND LORD OF LORDS.

And I saw an angel standing in the sun; and he cried with a loud voice, saying to all the fowls that fly in the midst of heaven, Come and gather yourselves together unto the supper of the great God; that ye may eat the flesh of kings, and the flesh of captains, and the flesh of mighty men, and the flesh of horses, and of them that sit on them, and the flesh of all men, both free and bond, both small and great.

And I saw the beast, and the kings of the earth, and their armies, gathered together to make war against him that sat on the horse, and against his army.

And the beast was taken, and with him the false prophet that wrought miracles before him, with which he deceived them that had received the mark of the beast, and them that worshipped his image. These both were cast alive into a lake of fire burning with brimstone.

And the remnant were slain with the sword of him that sat upon the horse, which sword proceeded out of his mouth: and all the fowls were filled with their flesh.

The Marriage Supper of the Lamb

Chapter 19 is the beginning of the marriage of Jesus Christ to His bride, the people of God. All followers of Christ who have ever lived sit down with Jesus face to face in the marriage supper of the Lamb. The beast and the false prophet have been cast into the lake of fire. And our Lord Jesus Christ completely takes over. This is the moment when righteousness fully triumphs.

Revelation 20:1-6

And I saw an angel come down from heaven, having the key of the bottomless pit and a great chain in his hand. And he laid hold on the dragon, that old serpent, which is the Devil, and Satan, and bound him a thousand years, and cast him into the bottomless pit, and shut him up, and set a seal upon him, that he should deceive the nations no more, till the thousand years should be fulfilled: and after that he must be loosed a little season.

And I saw thrones, and they sat upon them, and judgment was given unto them: and I saw the souls of them that were beheaded for the witness of Jesus, and for the word of God, and which had not

worshipped the beast, neither his image, neither had received his
mark upon their foreheads, or in their hands; and they lived and
reigned with Christ a thousand years.

But the rest of the dead lived not again until the thousand years
were finished. This is the first resurrection. Blessed and holy is he
that hath part in the first resurrection: on such the second death hath
no power, but they shall be priests of God and of Christ, and shall
reign with him a thousand years.

The Millennial Reign

We are told that during this 1,000-year period, the devil will be
bound in the bottomless pit. This is what is called the millennial
reign. Millennium means 1,000 years. John sees that during the
1,000-year period, the people who sit upon the thrones are very
active, for judgment is given unto them.

We are also told that this is the first resurrection. All the people
of God who have lived and died (until the time of Armageddon when
Christ returns) are raised in this first resurrection. And they are
called blessed because the second death has no power over them.

You see, the first death is a physical death. But the second death
is the death, or eternal punishment, of the body, mind, and spirit.
Those who are raised in the first resurrection will be priests of God
and will reign with Him a thousand years. But all who have died in
sin from the beginning of creation will not live again until the
thousand years are over, at which time they will come to judgment.

Revelation 20:7-15

And when the thousand years are expired, Satan shall be loosed out
of his prison, and shall go out to deceive the nations which are in
the four quarters of the earth, Gog and Magog, to gather them together
to battle: the number of whom is as the sand of the sea.

And they went up on the breadth of the earth, and compassed the
camp of the saints about, and the beloved city: and fire came down
from God out of heaven, and devoured them. And the devil that
deceived them was cast into the lake of fire and brimstone, where
the beast and the false prophet are, and shall be tormented day and
night for ever and ever.

And I saw a great white throne, and him that sat on it, from whose
face the earth and the heaven fled away; and there was found no
place for them. And I saw the dead, small and great, stand before
God; and the books were opened: and another book was opened,
which is the book of life: and the dead were judged out of those things

which were written in the books, according to their works.

And the sea gave up the dead which were in it; and death and hell delivered up the dead which were in them: and they were judged every man according to their works. And death and hell were cast into the lake of fire. This is the second death. And whosoever was not found written in the book of life was cast into the lake of fire.

The Final End of Satan

The question arises, due to the final deception of humanity by Satan, "Will Christ not destroy, in the battle of Armageddon, everything that is unlike God?" First of all, when Jesus Christ comes back the second time, He will bring with Him His saints. But there will be some people who accepted Christ during the tribulation period and did not die, who will be on the earth when Christ returns the second time.

It is my personal opinion that these people will have children during the millennial reign. Therefore, the children of this period will be born with the seed of sin in their hearts, just as people are today. These children also will not have a tempter coming against them to test their free moral agency and their power of choice, because the devil will be in the bottomless pit.

Because of these factors there must be a final testing of the free moral agency of mankind. So the devil will be released for a little season. He will tempt all the people on the earth and many will yield to him, showing that sin never changes. He will gather all of his followers into an army and will come against the city of God, the great Jerusalem that will come down from above. But at the height of the war, fire will descend from God and devour the army. This is the final end. For the devil will be cast into the lake of fire, where Antichrist and the false prophet are, and will be tormented day and night forever and ever. The earth and humanity will finally be free from the devil and his evil. Hallelujah!

Revelation 21:1-3

And I saw a new heaven and a new earth: for the first heaven and the first earth were passed away; and there was no more sea. And I John saw the holy city, new Jerusalem, coming down from God out of heaven, prepared as a bride adorned for her husband.

And I heard a great voice out of heaven saying, Behold, the tabernacle of God is with men, and he will dwell with them, and they shall be his people, and God himself shall be with them, and be their God.

What we just read describes what God originally had in mind when he placed Adam and Eve in the Garden of Eden. Oh, how it would have been if Adam had not rebelled! I am looking forward to that day when we will once again have full communion and fellowship with God our Creator.

Revelation 21:4-8

And God shall wipe away all tears from their eyes; and there shall be no more death, neither sorrow, nor crying, neither shall there be any more pain: for the former things are passed away.

And he that sat upon the throne said, Behold, I make all things new. And he said unto me, Write: for these words are true and faithful. And he said unto me, It is done. I am Alpha and Omega, the beginning and the end. I will give unto him that is athirst of the fountain of the water of life freely.

He that overcometh shall inherit all things; and I will be his God, and he shall be my son.

But the fearful, and unbelieving, and the abominable, and murderers, and whoremongers, and sorcerers, and idolaters, and all liars, shall have their part in the lake which burneth with fire and brimstone: which is the second death.

The Second Death

People who die without Christ experience their first death. They remain in hell until the end of the thousand years and then are brought forth to the judgment. After the judgment they are cast into the lake of fire and brimstone with Antichrist, the false prophet, and the devil. That is the second death.

Revelation 21:9-27

And there came unto me one of the seven angels which had the seven vials full of the seven last plagues, and talked with me, saying, Come hither, I will shew thee the bride, the Lamb's wife.

And he carried me away in the spirit to a great and high mountain, and shewed me that great city, the holy Jerusalem, descending out of heaven from God, having the glory of God: and her light was like unto a stone most precious, even like a jasper stone, clear as crystal; and had a wall great and high, and had twelve gates, and at the gates twelve angels, and names written thereon, which are the names of the twelve tribes of the children of Israel: on the east three gates; on the north three gates; on the south three gates; and on the west three gates. And the wall of the city had twelve foundations, and in them the names of the twelve apostles of the Lamb.

And he that talked with me had a golden reed to measure the city, and the gates thereof, and the wall thereof. And the city lieth foursquare, and the length is as large as the breadth: and he measured the city with the reed, twelve thousand furlongs. The length and the breadth and the height of it are equal.

And he measured the wall thereof, an hundred and forty and four cubits, according to the measure of a man, that is, of the angel. And the building of the wall of it was of jasper: and the city was pure gold, like unto clear glass.

And the foundations of the wall of the city were garnished with all manner of precious stones. The first foundation was jasper; the second, sapphire; the third, a chalcedony; the fourth, an emerald; the fifth, sardonyx; the sixth, sardius; the seventh, chrysolyte; the eighth, beryl; the ninth, a topaz; the tenth, a chrysoprasus; the eleventh, a jacinth; the twelfth, an amethyst.

And the twelve gates were twelve pearls; every several gate was of one pearl: and the street of the city was pure gold, as it were transparent glass. And I saw no temple therein: for the Lord God Almighty and the Lamb are the temple of it.

And the city had no need of the sun, neither of the moon, to shine in it: for the glory of God did lighten it, and the Lamb is the light thereof. And the nations of them which are saved shall walk in the light of it: and the kings of the earth do bring their glory and honour into it.

And the gates of it shall not be shut at all by day: for there shall be no night there. And they shall bring the glory and honour of the nations into it. And there shall in no wise enter into it any thing that defileth, neither whatsoever worketh abomination, or maketh a lie: but they which are written in the Lamb's book of life.

The "Heaven" of Heaven

In Verse 7 the Lord says something very special to us. He says, "He that overcometh shall inherit all things." This does not mean a mere passive serving of the Lord. It means an activeness in Christ's work. It means being a witness of the Lord.

John describes the city of God as being 1,500 miles in height and length on each side. It is a perfect square. And it is adorned with all types of precious stones. The things people fight over and even kill for today are there in such abundance that it is beyond our human comprehension. But the important thing about it is that far beyond just the beauty of the city, the Lord God and the Lamb are the temple of the city of God. Just as God walked and talked with Adam and Eve in the Garden of Eden, so He will be restored to His rightful place as the temple of His people.

Of course, it will be great to walk on the streets of gold and see the glorious things of God. But the "heaven" of heaven is the Lord. In other words, heaven is heaven because of God. Everything else is built around Him because He is the source. There is one thing I hope you and I will learn for good — that God was, is, and always will be our source.

Revelation 22:1-7

And he shewed me a pure river of water of life, clear as crystal, proceeding out of the throne of God and of the Lamb. In the midst of the street of it, and on either side of the river, was there the tree of life, which bare twelve manner of fruits, and yielded her fruit every month: and the leaves of the tree were for the healing of the nations.

And there shall be no more curse: but the throne of God and of the Lamb shall be in it; and his servants shall serve him: and they shall see his face; and his name shall be in their foreheads.

And there shall be no night there; and they need no candle, neither light of the sun; for the Lord God giveth them light: and they shall reign for ever and ever.

And he said unto me, These sayings are faithful and true: and the Lord God of the holy prophets sent his angel to shew unto his servants the things which must shortly be done. Behold, I come quickly; blessed is he that keepeth the sayings of the prophecy of this book.

The Sudden Coming of the Lord

Many of us ask what it means when Christ says, "Behold, I come quickly." I personally believe He is saying, "Behold, I come suddenly." He is not setting a calendar date for His return. He is saying, "When I come, it will be a sudden coming." Remember that Jesus said during His lifetime that His coming would be as a thief in the night, when people are not physically prepared for the thief. So, He is saying, "I will come suddenly."

I want to be prepared for the suddenness of His return. But I must build, work, and pray until then. For Jesus said, "Occupy until I come." I cannot give you the day, week, month, or year when Jesus will return. And neither can anyone else. Jesus said, "Of that day and hour, no man knoweth, not even the angels, but My Father only." It will catch the world unawares. And it will catch us unawares unless we are occupying, overcoming, and obeying the prophetic message of this book.

Revelation 22:8-10

And I John saw these things, and heard them. And when I had heard and seen, I fell down to worship before the feet of the angel which shewed me these things. Then saith he unto me, See thou do it not: for I am thy fellowservant, and of thy brethren the prophets, and of them which keep the sayings of this book: worship God.

And he saith unto me, Seal not the sayings of the prophecy of this book: for the time is at hand.

God is summing it all up and He wants John to reveal it to the world. He says, "Do not seal the prophecy of this book and lay it aside on a shelf. You reveal it because the time is at hand for it to be known to the world." God is saying to him, "Get the word out."

Revelation 22:11-19

He that is unjust, let him be unjust still: and he which is filthy, let him be filthy still: and he that is righteous, let him be righteous still: and he that is holy, let him be holy still. And, behold, I come quickly; and my reward is with me, to give every man according as his work shall be. I am Alpha and Omega, the beginning and the end, the first and the last.

Blessed are they that do his commandments, that they may have right to the tree of life, and may enter in through the gates into the city. For without are dogs, and sorcerers, and whoremongers, and murderers, and idolaters, and whosoever loveth and maketh a lie.

I Jesus have sent mine angel to testify unto you these things in the churches. I am the root and the offspring of David, and the bright and morning star.

And the Spirit and the bride say, Come. And let him that heareth say, Come. And let him that is athirst come. And whosoever will, let him take the water of life freely.

For I testify unto every man that heareth the words of the prophecy of this book, If any man shall add unto these things, God shall add unto him the plagues that are written in this book: and if any man shall take away from the words of the book of this prophecy, God shall take away his part out of the book of life, and out of the holy city, and from the things which are written in this book.

I think John is speaking primarily to the people who will copy the scroll of Revelation. They did not have the printing press then, so scribes had to copy by hand books that were to be reproduced.

John is saying to them, "Do not change these words. Do not change the codes God has given me in this book." And he is saying to all people of all ages, "Be careful about trying to cancel out these visions."

Revelation 22:20,21

He which testifieth these things saith, Surely I come quickly. Amen. Even so, come, Lord Jesus.

The grace of our Lord Jesus Christ be with you all. Amen.

A Special Closing

"The grace of our Lord Jesus Christ be with you." Paul often closed his books with these words. It was the way the early Christians closed their church services. When they wrote letters to one another, they closed by saying these words. And before I pray my final prayer with you, I want to close the book of Revelation and the New Testament by saying these very special words: "The grace of our Lord Jesus Christ be with you, Partner. Amen."

Father, we have completed Your entire New Testament. We have felt the anointing of Your Holy Spirit all the way through, even during those most difficult passages. We have soared like the eagle during those glorious times when the truth of Your Word has shone in our hearts. And we thank You, Lord, that You have been with us and have revealed Your Word to us.

Dear partner, I pray for God to bless you. I pray your heart will be open and overflowing with love for God. I pray you will make a quality decision to obey God, to keep His commandments, to carry out His Holy Word, to be His witness. I pray that no matter what comes or goes, how hard or easy it may be, whether people are for you or against you, and no matter how the devil comes against your life, that you will know that you know that you know that Jesus lives in you and therefore you are a winner. You are more than a conqueror through Jesus Christ who loves and died for you. And Jesus bless you, heal you, and keep you forever. Amen and amen.

Index

Index

Nathan, i. 245
Nathanael, i. 391
Nazarenes, ii. 136
Nebuchadnezzar, i. 9
Need for Redeemer, iii. 72
Needs, i. 295, 301, 302, 315, 316
Neighbor, i. 305
Nero, iii. 3, 47, 48, 56, 106, 111
New covenant (see: Covenant, new)
New creatures, ii. 338
Nicodemus, i. 395, 396, 477
Noah, i. 335
Noonday darkness, i. 231
Numerology, i. 4, 5, 483; ii. 259; iii. 108, 109, 125, 146

O_____
Obedience, i. 20, 121, 136, 137, 142, 160, 161, 174-176, 246, 248, 277, 310, 392, 409, 410, 431, 432, 485; ii. 5, 6, 30, 90, 91, 125, 143, 344, 379, 386, 464; iii. 49
Occult, ii. 51
Old covenant (see: Covenant, old)
Old Testament, i. 374, 375
Olive tree, iii. 132
  and grafted branches, ii. 206
Omnipotent, i. 17, 38, 59, 60, 140, 141, 174-176, 185, 186, 270, 371, 438, 469, 470; iii. 101
Omnipresent, i. 282; ii. 150, 151
Omniscient, i. 17, 140, 141; ii. 188
One-eyed chicken, i. 216
Onesimus, ii. 469-471
Onesiphorus, ii. 451
Open-minded, i. 273, 308, 309, 463; ii. 106
Opposition, i. 284, 285; ii. 93
Oral Roberts Ministries, ii. 5, 6, 74, 89, 96
Oral Roberts University, ii. 37,

239, 250, 305
Order of administration, ii. 284, 285
Order of creation, ii. 267
Organization, i. 184, 185
Orphans, iii. 36
Overcoming, ii. 418; iii. 136

P_____
Papyrus, ii. 327
Parables, i. 86, 87, 120, 121, 173
Paradise, i. 332, 333; ii. 315, 380
Paralytic healed, i. 165, 166
Passion, ii. 253, 453
Passover, i. 220, 360; ii. 9
Pastor(s), ii. 381
Paul, i. 4, 27, 241, 242, 383, 462; ii. 3, 39, 42, 47, 48, 58, 60, 61, 76, 82-84, 87, 90, 92, 95, 96, 104, 105, 109, 122, 132, 159, 222, 234, 235, 253, 258, 269, 314, 348, 354, 389, 398, 410, 417, 455; iii. 3, 5, 66
  and Barnabas divide, ii. 99
  and Mosaic Law, ii. 128, 129
  and Silas in prison, ii. 103
  at Athens, ii. 107
  at Thessalonica, ii. 415
  before Jewish council, ii. 133, 134
  bitten by snake, ii. 151, 152
  exorcises a demon, ii. 102
  flees Damascus, ii. 60
  in Corinth, ii. 111
  in Ephesus, ii. 118, 119
  in Jerusalem, ii. 128
  in prison, ii. 394, 451, 452
  in Rome, ii. 154, 155
  in the temple, ii. 129
  meets Roman Christians, ii. 153
  on Mars Hill, ii. 108
  preached to Gentiles, ii. 220
  prisoner in Caesarea, ii. 139
  speaks to mob, ii. 130-132